BOB SORGE

Dealing with the Rejection and Praise of Man

Third Printing (2002)

Other books by Bob Sorge:
• ENVY: THE ENEMY WITHIN
• SECRETS OF THE SECRET PLACE
• GLORY: WHEN HEAVEN INVADES EARTH
• PAIN, PERPLEXITY AND PROMOTION: A prophetic interpretation of the book of Job
• THE FIRE OF GOD'S LOVE
• THE FIRE OF DELAYED ANSWERS
• IN HIS FACE: A prophetic call to renewed focus
• EXPLORING WORSHIP: A practical guide to praise and worship
• Exploring Worship WORKBOOK & DISCUSSION GUIDE

DEALING WITH THE REJECTION AND PRAISE OF MAN
Copyright © 1999 by Bob Sorge
Published by Oasis House
P.O. Box 127
Greenwood, Missouri 64034-0127

www.oasishouse.net

Edited by Edie Veach.

Printed in the United States of America
Library of Congress Catalog Card Number: 99-075868
International Standard Book Number: 0-9621185-8-3

Preface

There are two primary ways we are healed from the wounds of past rejections:

1) Through a sovereign work of grace administered to our hearts by the power of the Holy Spirit. As we confess our sins (especially of bitterness and anger) and willfully forgive those who have wronged us, the Holy Spirit rushes in to restore areas of our soul that were damaged. We may not know how God did it, we just know that His grace has cleansed us.

2) Through the illumination of truth to our minds. When the truth of God's word finds good soil in our hearts, it lodges within us and renews our minds (Romans 12:2). We begin to experience the power of Jesus' promise, "'And you shall know the truth, and the truth shall make you free'" (John 8:32). God's truth has the power to liberate us from the entangling cords of past rejections.

The purpose of this book is to deal with this second dynamic—to minister wholeness and freedom through truth.

This is not a book of easy answers. These truths will search the depths of your inner attitudes and motives. I'm convinced that if you will join me in making these truths your personal pursuit, you will embark on the pathway of ever-increasing freedom in your walk with Christ. "But the path of the just is like the shining sun, that shines ever brighter unto the perfect day" (Proverbs 4:18).

Come with me to God's word with a prayerful, expectant heart. Healing and freedom will come as you meekly receive the truths of God's word set forth in this book. Let God's truth set you free from the power of rejection's woundings and from the entrapment of man's praises.

The rejection of man and the praise of man can be equally deadly traps. Virtually all of us struggle with both pitfalls. The truths that set us free from both extremes are amazingly similar.

Important: Start with Chapter One, and read this book in its sequential order. The truths in this book build on each other, and that benefit will be lost if you start in the middle or last chapter.

Bob Sorge
Kansas City, Missouri
August, 1999

Contents

Chapter 1

Rejection:
The Universal Malady

You have felt rejected. I have felt rejected. To one degree or another, every single one of us has tasted the pain of feeling rejection from other people.

Our world is filled with rejection:

- Babies are unwanted by their mothers.
- Children are assaulted or abused by their parents.
- People curse and rail upon each other.
- People are mocked for their physical or mental qualities.
- Others are robbed, raped, swindled, and even murdered.
- Friends discard friends.
- Divorce rips families apart.
- Shrewd business dealings violate victims.
- Nations declare war on each other.
- And the list goes on and on.

Even in happy circumstances we encounter rejection. You may have grown up in a two-parent family with a stable emotional environment and a middle class lifestyle, but you have still been rejected. Every human being knows what it is to feel rejection.

Because of our brokenness through sin, we humans are particularly adroit at dispensing rejection. And our sinful fallenness also makes us susceptible to receiving rejection when none is intended.

Rejection is an experience that is so universally understood that it requires no definition. We all know what it means. Rejection can take many forms—hurtful words, withdrawn attention, unspoken gestures, unreciprocated love, malicious assault, etc. When we're hurt by others, we don't always label it clearly as rejection, but even when we haven't analyzed the incident fully or precisely, the pain is still very real.

Rejection hurts.

God has created into the fabric of our humanness the desire to be accepted and loved. When we feel rejection (the opposite of love and acceptance), we instinctively fight to regain our emotional balance. We process and rehearse the experience repeatedly in our minds, trying to find a way to cope and insulate ourselves from the pain.

Processing The Pain

All of us have searched for ways to shield ourselves from rejection, or to find resolve from the pain of past hurts.

I once found a letter that put a creative twist on this business of dealing with rejection. This letter caught my attention because it reminded me of the many rejections my brother Sheldon experienced when he completed his doctorate. He had studied so that he could teach at the university level. Upon graduation, he sent out scores of applications to universities across the nation, hoping to get hired. What he got, instead, was a host of responses that are commonly known as "rejection letters." Students of post-graduate education will nearly kill themselves to earn a degree, often to then experience rejection upon rejection as they search the job market.

This letter is the fictitious response of a graduate who applied to many universities for a teaching position. After receiving a plethora of the standardized rejections, he finally became exasperated to the point of writing this response to one of the universities:

> **Dear Professor Worthington,**
>
> **Thank you for your letter of March 23. After careful consideration, I regret to inform you that I am unable to accept your refusal to offer me an assistant professor position in your department.**
>
> **This year I have been particularly fortunate in receiving an unusually large number of rejection letters. With such a varied and promising field of opportunities, it is impossible for me to accept all refusals.**
>
> **Despite Whitson University's outstanding qualifications and previous experience in rejecting applicants, I find that your rejection does not meet my needs at this time. Therefore, I will assume the position of assistant professor in your department this August. I look forward to seeing you then.**
>
> **Best of luck in rejecting future applicants.**
>
> **Sincerely,**
> **TJ Baggins**

Wouldn't it be nice if rejection were this easy to process? A simple shrug of the shoulders, a quick retort that "your rejection does not meet my needs at this time," and then a backhanded dismissal of the pain. Poof—gone!

But it ain't that easy.

The Pain Of Rejection

Rejection affects us more profoundly than we care to admit. We can convince ourselves that we have not been wounded by someone's rejection, but then we begin to realize we have constructed self-protecting mechanisms to insulate ourselves from recurrences of that kind of injury. The protective walls we build around our souls are the evidence that the rejection has wounded us more than we thought. Consequently, our relationships with others suffer. We have distanced ourselves from others because of our past pains, and now struggle to find full satisfaction in the relationships God has given us. Rejection has left its scar.

It's tempting to respond to rejection with an inner vow: "That's the last time I'll let anyone else hurt me like that." We think we're protecting ourselves from further rejection, but instead we're trapping ourselves in a pattern of behavior that only binds us to the bitterness of the past. When we serve that need to stay protected, we relate to others in a way that only serves to escalate the volume of rejection we continue to encounter from them.

Once we've been really wounded by rejection, relationships become a great risk. We calculate, "Are the potential benefits of this relationship worth risking the potential hurts of this relationship?" So we decide how much of our soul we will open to this person. New relationships can be seen as a gamble.

Even marriage can be a gamble. We think we've found someone we can finally trust, so we get married. We open ourselves and make ourselves vulnerable to our spouse. And then we discover that we often suffer the greatest wounds of rejection from those who love us most!

I Connect With This Subject

I am not writing about rejection from a position of objective aloofness. I have had to wrestle personally with processing rejection from other Christians, and have also had to face the pain of realizing that many others have felt rejected by me. When God began to teach me about rejection, He did it through both means—through allowing me to feel rejected, and through allowing me to cause others to feel rejected through my imperfect attempts to relate to them.

When I consider those from whom I have felt rejection, I can't think of a single one who purposefully intended to hurt me. And when I think of those who have felt rejected by me, I can't think of a single person that I meant to hurt. I was not malicious toward them, they were not malicious toward me. We weren't trying to hurt and reject each other, in fact our intentions were to love one another. But rejection just seemed to happen anyways.

Sometimes we are rejected by others. And sometimes we feel rejected when in fact we're being accepted. Either way, the feelings of rejection are the result of our broken humanity, our fallenness, our ineptitude at relating to one another in the perfection of Christ. Furthermore, it's possible to relate to someone absolutely perfectly—as Jesus related to the Pharisees—and have them feel rejected by you.

I began to awaken to the reality that a growing number of people in my sphere of influence have felt rejected by me. When I began to count them, I became alarmed at how large the list was! I can't think of a single instance when I meant to reject any of them. In some cases, I knew I would be interpreted as rejecting them; in other cases I was taken by surprise at their responses. In fact, I've known the frustrating syndrome of sincerely thinking that I was expressing particular acceptance and affirmation toward someone, only to discover later that they received my words as a rejection.

I have also tasted a little bit of what the apostle Paul wrote about when he told the believers at Corinth, "And I will very gladly spend and be spent for your souls; though the more abundantly I love you, the less I am loved" (2 Corinthians 12:15). Paul loved the Corinthians so much that he was willing to hazard their affection in order to minister loving correction and rebuke. He extended genuine love to them, but because of their immaturity they interpreted his love as rejection. This is one of the risks of spiritual fatherhood. When God calls us to spiritual oversight, there are times when our spiritual children feel that we are being less than loving. They're not able to see, however, that we're loving them more than ever. Parenting occasionally means that our children reject us because of the stance we must take.

In our better moments, with the best of intentions, we can still cause others to feel rejected by us. As long as we're on this earth, rejection will always be one of the foremost issues involved in the dynamics of our interpersonal relationships.

We've all known rejection in the past. And we're all on a pathway to a future which has the letters "REJECTION" emblazoned brightly overhead. It's inevitable; we are guaranteed to feel rejected again. Thus, how we deal with rejection becomes an ever-present issue which we must face honestly and practically.

A Vast Subject

Dealing with the rejection and praise of man is a very diverse and intricate topic. Every one of us has unique circumstances and situations that we're trying to process. Someone reading this book might think at certain points, "Okay, I understand what you're saying, but you're not really addressing what happened to me."

With a subject as vast as this, it's impossible to address every possible scenario where there's been rejection or the praise of man. So rather than focusing on specific situations, we will emphasize general principles.

If this teaching surfaces a question relative to your own specific circumstances, and you find the material in this book incomplete, I would direct you to the words of Jesus who said, "Go and learn what this means" (Matthew 9:13). Jesus told His listeners to do their own Bible study.

So be encouraged, you have the Holy Spirit who has been given to you to guide you into all truth. Take the Scriptures and principles covered in this book into your study chamber, and believe that the Holy Spirit will help you uncover the specific answers you need for your own unique circumstances.

Although this book is limited in its scope, I pray it will help provide direction in your pursuit of God's heart. Come with me now as we begin to look at this fascinating subject.

Chapter 2

Even Jesus Experienced Rejection

The Bible is chock-full of stories about people who were rejected by others. Some of the godliest people in the Bible experienced the most rejection of anyone. Not the least of those was Jesus Christ Himself.

Jesus Was Rejected

"The heart knows its own bitterness" (Proverbs 14:10). No one but you knows the depths of your own heartache. You have known the bitterness of rejection, the depths of which no other human being fully understands. You have carried the wounds of a private pain, suffering in a way known to God alone. However, Proverbs 4:10 doesn't just refer to us; it also refers to God. Only God knows His own bitterness. No one really knows the bitterness of heart that God has experienced over the betrayal of Lucifer and his angels. And no one but Jesus knows His bitterness of soul over the mutiny of mankind.

No one understands rejection better than Jesus.

The prophet foretold that He would be "rejected by men" (Isaiah 53:3), and the gospel writers give us ample evidence of how that was fulfilled. John wrote, "He came to His own, and His own did not receive Him" (John 1:11). Jesus said, "If the world hates you, you know that it hated Me before it hated you" (John 15:18).

On one occasion, shortly after He commenced His earthly ministry, He stopped in on His hometown of Nazareth. The people of Nazareth had known Jesus since His childhood, so they were cynical toward His message and ministry. Jesus articulated the truth that prophets are not without honor except in their own hometown. When He illustrated that truth from the Scriptures, His neighborhood buddies became instantly irate, and taking Him to the brow of a hill they tried to throw Him down the cliff. Jesus escaped, but He doubtless felt the sting of His childhood friends' rejection.

Jesus' life illustrates a simple truth: even if you're *perfect*, you'll still experience rejection.

His greatest rejection came from the religious leaders of the day—the scribes, Pharisees, Sadducees, and lawyers (those who interpreted legal matters related to Moses' law). The following passage is just one example among many:

> *And as He said these things to them, the scribes and the Pharisees began to assail Him vehemently, and to cross-examine Him about many things, lying in wait for Him, and seeking to catch Him in something He might say, that they might accuse Him* (Luke 11:53-54).

Now, I call that rejection!

Somebody once said, "When I become more like Jesus, maybe I won't be rejected so much." The truth is the exact opposite! The more you become like Jesus, the more rejection you will know.

So establish your heart now in the expectation that, as you become more like Him, you will face even more rejection in the days ahead. Now, just because you're being rejected doesn't necessarily mean it's because you're being Christlike. But be assured that as you become more Christlike, you will taste of ever-increasing rejection. "Yes, and all who desire to live godly in Christ Jesus will suffer persecution" (2 Timothy 3:12).

Jeremiah's Rejection

Jesus was said to be like Jeremiah, and perhaps there was no Old Testament prophet who suffered more rejection than Jeremiah. He prophesied faithfully what God gave him, but as a result virtually everyone seemed to hate him. Jeremiah vented his pain when he wrote, "Woe is me, my mother, that you have borne me, a man of strife and a man of contention to the whole earth! I have neither lent for interest, nor have men lent to me for interest. Every one of them curses me" (Jeremiah 15:10). He is saying that he has wronged no one, but they all curse him anyways because of the prophetic word he has delivered in the name of the Lord.

This was a very painful experience for Jeremiah, which he confirms in the following verses:

> *Your words were found, and I ate them, and Your word was to me the joy and rejoicing of my heart; for I am called by Your name, O LORD God of hosts. I did not sit in the assembly of the mockers, nor did I rejoice; I sat alone because of Your hand, for You have filled me with indignation. Why is my pain perpetual and my wound incurable, which refuses to be healed? Will You surely be to me like an unreliable stream, as waters that fail?* (Jeremiah 15:16-18).

Jeremiah was saying that he "sat alone" in social isolation because of the stigma he carried over his life message. The only joy in his life was the word of the Lord, which he willingly ate (took in to himself). He was in constant pain because of his loneliness and reproach, and he even questioned if God's earlier promises to him were going to be fulfilled.

God's response to Jeremiah was, "Thus says the LORD: 'If you return, then I will bring you back; you shall stand before Me; if you take out the precious from the vile, you shall be as My mouth'" (Jeremiah 15:19). God was saying, "If you will return from your place of doubt and self-preoccupation, you will stand in My immediate presence, face to face with Me. You will behold My face, and you will be My mouthpiece." This was an awesome calling, but the pricetag for Jeremiah was untold rejection from his compatriots.

Was Jeremiah's reward worth the rejection he experienced? Actually, the full impact of the reward for his faithfulness was not seen in his lifetime. The reward of his consecration was not to be fully evident until the coming of Christ. We see it finally in these words from Matthew's gospel: "When Jesus came into the region of Caesarea Philippi, He asked His disciples, saying, 'Who do men say that I, the Son of Man, am?' So they said, 'Some say John the Baptist, some Elijah, and others Jeremiah or one of the prophets'" (Matthew 16:13-14). Jesus had known such widespread rejection that the people said He was like Jeremiah. The disciples were saying, "When the people look at You, Jesus, some of them say you remind them of Jeremiah." What an awesome epitaph! Imagine the swell of Jeremiahs' heart when he heard those words.

The people were not saying, "Jeremiah reminds us of Jesus." They were saying, "Jesus reminds us of Jeremiah." When they looked at how much rejection Jesus was experiencing, the people said He reminded them of Jeremiah. This was the capstone on Jeremiah's reward. Rejection is never enjoyable, but I am suggesting that *any* amount of rejection is worth that kind of affirmation! O to look like Jesus!

The Reward Of Rejection

When we embrace rejection as Jesus did and resolve ourselves to face rejection for the sake of His name, we share in the reward of that reproach. **Earthly rejection, properly embraced, is an opportunity to gain heavenly treasure.**

The Scriptures use the pearl as a brilliant example of this truth. Pearl is the natural substance an oyster produces when it is afflicted from an outside source. When a gritty grain of sand settles into a crevice inside an oyster's shell, located in such a way that the oyster cannot dislodge it through its natural means of squirting out water, the oyster has a backup system for dealing with the irritant. It secretes a substance that produces a soft, smooth coating around the grain of sand—a substance called pearl. Over time, layer upon layer is added. Eventually, that which vexed and pained the oyster is the very thing which produces something of great value and beauty.

In the same way, pearl is used in Scripture to describe the eternal treasure that trials and crises produce in us. Jesus said, "Do not give what is holy to the dogs; nor cast your pearls before swine, lest they trample them under their feet, and turn and tear you in pieces" (Matthew 7:6). What He means is, "Don't take those valuable lessons you learned in the fire, those precious things you gained while being refined in the crucible of rejection, and then just spill them to any undiscerning person. If you're not careful, you can take something that you've learned in the crisis season and share it with the wrong person, and instead of them being blessed by the preciousness of what you've gained, they despise what you say and demean that which you cherish."

Jesus intends that we turn our pains into pearls. This pearl is very beautiful in His sight but is despised by the undiscerning.

The Book Of Revelation describes the gates of heaven in this way: "The twelve gates were twelve pearls: each individual gate was of one pearl" (Revelation 21:21). In other words, we enter the heavenly city through gates of pearl. There is only one way to get to heaven, and that is by turning the trials of life into eternal treasure (pearl). The apostles attested to this when they said, "We must through many tribulations enter the kingdom of God" (Acts 14:22).

Jesus is looking for a bride with this kind of pearly character. He pointed to this in one of His parables: "Again, the kingdom of heaven is like a merchant seeking beautiful pearls, who, when he had found one pearl of great price, went and sold all that he had and bought it" (Matthew 13:45-46). Jesus Himself is the merchant who, when He found one pearl of superior value, sold everything in order to purchase it. That pearl of great value is the bride of Christ—the people of God—those who came through great tribulation, but who turned the pains of life into pearl. The price He paid was His death on the cross, which redeemed us to Himself. Jesus looks at His redeemed bride as "one pearl of great price," and He is totally awestruck by her. He looks at her dazzling glory and says, "Wow! She's beautiful!"

Not one creature in the pantheons of heaven's hosts has tasted of the same rejection that the Son of God has known —not one, that is, except His bride. His heart is drawn in incredible affection toward this bride who has shared in His sufferings. Surely, any rejection in this life is worth embracing properly in order to be attractive to our beloved Bridegroom in the last day because of our shared experiences and hardships!

Chapter 3

Rejection: God's Specialty Tool

At the Master's workbench, where He forms His servants into the image of Christ, there are many tools at His disposal for fashioning character development. There is one tool which He uses in a singularly powerful way, however, to accelerate the maturity of His chosen vessels, and yes, that tool is called "Rejection."

Rejection is one of God's specialty tools in the school of the Spirit. When God takes a particular liking to a saint, He fashions that saint by surrounding him with unusual doses of rejection.

Job is a great example of this truth. Because of God's affection for Job, God used rejection in a profound way to shape Job's character while he was in the crucible. The rejection that Job received from his friends, family, and acquaintances was designed by God as a necessary part of the process to bring him forward into effective spiritual fatherhood. I pursue that thought further in my book on Job *(PAIN, PERPLEXITY, AND PROMOTION: A prophetic interpretation of the book of Job)*.

When God destines a saint for extraordinary influence in the body of Christ, He prepares him through the rejection of people. If that saint is to become a compassionate servant-leader, he will first need to drink deeply of the lacerating sting of rejection. This will tenderize him to the reality of rejection, and help sensitize him to how easily rejection can be inflicted upon others. Because of his sensitivity in this area, the servant-leader will handle the flock of God with exceptional care and tenderness. **It is to these sensitized shepherds that God can entrust greater influence.**

God took a man from the sheepfolds, and because of His unique delight in him He called him to be the shepherd of Israel. But to prepare him for that place of exceptional influence, God had to temper him with uncommon doses of rejection. I am referring to King David.

David's Rejections

Few men have experienced as much rejection as David did. Considering that God liked him so much, it's interesting to note how many people were bugged by him. Here's just a few examples of the kinds of rejection David experienced:

- When Samuel came to Jesse's home to anoint one of his sons as king of Israel, Jesse called all of his sons to the meeting—except his youngest son David. Jesse didn't even consider David to be a potential candidate! David got anointed by God anyways, yet he was smart enough to feel his father's rejection.
- When David was sent by his father to see how his brothers were doing on the battlefield, David got hit with rejection from his brothers. Eliab was still envious that David was the anointed of God, so when David came to visit them, we're told that, "Eliab his oldest brother heard when he spoke to the men; and Eliab's anger was aroused against David, and he said, 'Why did you come down here? And with whom have you left those few sheep in the wilderness? I know your pride and the insolence of your heart, for you have come down to see the battle'" (1 Samuel 17:28). Those are strong, stinging words of rejection.

- His father-in-law, King Saul, tried to kill him. Repeatedly. (I call that rejection!)
- His wife, Michal, despised him in her heart as he danced before the Lord. She said, "'How glorious was the king of Israel today, uncovering himself today in the eyes of the maids of his servants, as one of the base fellows shame-lessly uncovers himself!'" (2 Samuel 6:20). He's even getting rejection from his wife!
- Two of his very own sons whom he loved deeply (Absalom and Adonijah) attempted on separate occasions to overthrow their father, kill him, and take over his throne. The sting of rejection can't get much more personal and acute than that!

How did David process all this rejection? The evidence indicates that in the midst of these and many other rejections, David continually withdrew into the secret place and renewed his hope and confidence in God. He was able to keep perspective on all the rejections of men because he was receiving from the inside the explosive acceptance of his God. I can suppose David saying, "I can handle all this rejection when I have God's loving acceptance."

God Designs Rejection For Our Benefit

Although David was rejected by many people, the foremost personality in his life who illustrated the traumatizing effects of rejection was Absalom. Absalom epitomizes the rejection that comes against God's anointed servants.

Whenever there's a David, there's an Absalom spirit. It just goes with the territory. God uses Absalom's rejection to keep His Davids broken and contrite. All of us have the potential to be an Absalom, and all of us have the potential to be a David. Absalom felt rejected by his father, David, so he took revenge by seeking to usurp his father's sphere of authority. David felt rejected by Absalom, but he allowed that rejection to keep him soft and crying out to God. Because he responded properly to it, it was the rejection that seasoned David's soul and safeguarded him from tyrannical leadership.

A substantial step toward freedom of soul is made when we are able to see God as the author of life's rejections and not men. Although men are dispensing the rejection, God is actually allowing it in His sovereign plan for a divine purpose. The rejection is accomplishing something very profound in our soul and spirit. If we respond properly to it, the rejection will be used of God to shape and conform us into the image of Christ. Properly embraced, Absalom's rejection can become a gift.

When we feel the sting of men's rejection, as long as we perceive men as the source of the rejection, we will struggle in our attitudes toward them. Freedom begins to unfold when we realize that God designed their rejection for our personal benefit. So instead of struggling in our heart toward those who reject us, we can give thanks to God who allows it for a higher purpose.

Remember: If He *really* loves you, He'll craft some particularly painful rejection for you. Those God loves most are always rejected the most (e.g., Jesus, David, the prophets, and others). It's an essential element in God's process of character formation in the hearts of His servants.

It might be easy to think, "I'll be glad when I've passed the rejection test." Listen, David got rejection till his dying day! **Rejection is a vital ingredient in the training up of endtime leaders, and after we're trained and raised up it continues to be a necessary tool to maintain and guard our hearts in humility.** So prepare yourself. You'll never grow beyond the need for rejection to tenderize your heart before God.

When you view rejection as a gift from God to keep your heart pliable and dependent upon Him, you gain a new freedom in relating to people in love. Even though you know people are not dependable, you are able to give yourself to them in unqualified love, knowing that any rejection you receive from them is an opportunity for character development.

When people reject you, but you are fueled on the inside with the profound affections of your Father for you, then you're able to give yourself to your fellow man in love regardless of how he treats you. You can love again, knowing that eventually man will fail you. But you know that believer's sincerity, and you have profound faith in the grace of God at work in him or her. So you're able to love them without hypocrisy, even while you're fully aware of their frailty and weakness.

Chapter 4

The Real Source
of Healing

It's A Process

Learning to respond properly to rejection is a process that often takes many years. When we are newborn Christians, the Bible calls us "children." As children we don't handle rejection maturely, so the Lord challenges us to grow up into mature spiritual responses. This growth process is measured not simply in months but in years.

Children are often wounded most by rejection. Jesus was referring to children when He said, "'It is impossible that no offenses should come, but woe to him through whom they do come! It would be better for him if a millstone were hung around his neck, and he were thrown into the sea, than that he should offend one of these little ones'" (Luke 17:1-2).

Children don't have the tools to handle rejection right. It takes some children many years to come to terms with the rejection they've experienced. In the same way, as spiritual children, it can take us years to fully embrace all the truths in this area. I am a living example of that reality. Although I'm seeing some things and learning more and more how to respond to rejection, I'm still on a learning curve myself. And I expect to continue to learn for many years to come.

I say all this to say: give yourself time to master the principles of overcoming rejection. Christian maturity is not an instant attainment but rather a lifelong process.

Rejection can be viewed as a gift from God. The rejection of man has been the tool God has used to help many people see their spiritual bankruptcy, leading them to the foot of the cross in true repentance and faith. In such cases, thank God for rejection! **If we will allow it, rejection can drive us into the place of finding God.** Take as an example here the story of the fish who was rejected by the fisherman. The fisherman threw him back into the water because he was too small. The fish took a big rejection from that, especially since his older brother was lying on the bottom of the boat, all accepted by the fisherman. What the little fish didn't realize is that *the rejection was a blessing.* In a similar way, rejection from others can be a blessing if we will allow it to release us into kingdom truth and freedom. The simple truths in this book have the potential, through the power of the Holy Spirit, to help redeem the wounds of past rejections into kingdom pearls of blessing.

Now let's begin to look at the principles involved in responding redemptively to rejection.

The Source Of Healing

Jesus called rejection a trial. In the latter days of His earthly ministry He said to His disciples, "'But you are those who have continued with Me in My trials'" (Luke 22:28). We tend to look at Jesus' three years of ministry as incredibly exciting and awe-inspiring. Jesus, however, called them His "trials." Here we have a unique window on how He perceived His walk on earth. To Jesus, it was three years of pain. And the chief source of His pain was the incessant rejection that He faced from His detractors.

Jesus said rejection is a trial, a vexation to the soul. But even though Jesus was pained by rejection, He was never wounded in His soul by it. He was never embittered or offended by it. He had found a way to process rejection so that it stung Him without wounding Him.

Rejection hurts, but it need not wound. It's painful, but it doesn't have to penetrate the heart.

Rejection will always sting, but there is a healing balm. It is the unparalleled affection that the Father lavishes upon His children! No matter what the source of the rejection, nor the nature of the rejection, I have an internal wellspring of acceptance that flows from the heart of my heavenly Father to me.

He accepts me when others reject me. He accepts me, warts and all. He accepts me even when I blow it. He accepts me even while I sin. He accepts me regardless of my spiritual performance. He accepts me based upon the finished work of Christ's cross and His shed blood. I am as accepted by heaven as the only begotten Son of God Himself! When that acceptance is washing my soul on the inside, no amount of external rejection can wound me. I am constantly being healed by the everlasting affections of the Creator of the universe—who also happens to be my Father!

When we have been stung by rejection, we need to learn to retreat to the secret place, and be renewed and cleansed in the affections of our loving heavenly Father, the source of healing.

Rejection is a trial—but the acceptance of the Father is the healing ointment.

Forgiveness

One of the first steps to being healed from the ravages of rejection is by extending total forgiveness to those who have wronged us. There is so much to be said about forgiveness, and it is not within the purposes of this book to expand upon this truth. Many books have been written on the subject of forgiveness, and every Christian should master that subject. But let me make one brief point.

Jesus modelled true forgiveness when, at His crucifixion, He prayed, "Father, forgive them, for they do not know what they do" (Luke 23:34).

I used to think, "It was easy for Jesus to forgive His crucifiers because they were simply soldiers who were fol-

lowing orders." But a closer look gave me a different perspective. A careful reading of Jesus' trial and crucifixion reveals that the soldiers went far beyond their line of duty in
order to inflict pain and derision upon our Lord. They put a
crown of thorns upon Him, drove the thorns into His brow
with a rod, clothed Him with purple (the color of royalty),
mocked Him, and hit Him repeatedly. These Roman soldiers
hated their military appointment to Jerusalem. Dealing with
the Jews was a constant hassle, and it appears they vented
their angry frustrations upon this young Jew who seemed to
have a messiah complex. The soldiers far surpassed their
orders in maliciously violating Jesus, and yet He forgave
them!

But Jesus didn't merely forgive them. He took it to the
next step. He said, "Father, not only do I forgive them, but
I'm asking You to forgive them as well."

It's possible to forgive without taking it to the next step.
It's possible to forgive someone, but at the same time be thinking, "Just wait. Your turn is coming. There's a day of judgment coming. One day you're going to stand before the
throne of Almighty God. The secrets will come into the light,
and you will get yours! Oh, I forgive you; but one day you'll
pay!"

Jesus was saying, "Father, I'm asking You to blot out of
Your records in heaven this sin that they have committed
against Me. When they stand before You, may this sin not
even appear against them." This was also the prayer of
Stephen, the first Christian martyr, when he prayed while
being stoned to death for his faith, "Lord, do not charge them
with this sin" (Acts 7:60).

Now let's make this practical. Let's suppose, for example,
that your earthly father rejected you. Don't simply pray,
"Lord, I forgive my father." Say, "Lord, I'm asking you to
blot out of heaven's records every sin that my earthly father
ever committed against me. I forgive him, but now I ask You
to forgive him too." **When you release your offenders from
the judgment of their sin, you break the power of
unforgiveness and find a new release to relate in freedom
to others who sin against you.**

Accept Your Father's Love

The next step to becoming free from the power of rejection is in accepting your heavenly Father's love for you. When this love really touches your heart, it burns away the cords that rejection would bind around your heart.

But here's the key: *you must believe John 3:16!* "For God so loved the world that He gave His only begotten Son, that whoever believes in Him should not perish but have everlasting life." He loves you so much that He gave His one and only begotten Son—the Son that He loves so desperately— to the death of the cross. You must believe the good news that God loves you this much.

And once you believe this love, you must receive this love. If you will accept His passion for you, it will wash over you "in fathomless billows of love" (so said the old gospel song). His love will renew, saturate, strengthen, sustain, lift, and empower you. His love is the greatest power in the universe.

Your enemy, the devil, will do *anything* to hinder you from accepting and receiving this love. This is what Paul warned us about, "Now the Spirit expressly says that in latter times some will depart from the faith, giving heed to deceiving spirits and doctrines of demons" (1 Timothy 4:1). Demons want to deceive you into believing that God doesn't really love you this much. If you embrace these "doctrines of demons," you will "depart from the faith," from the confidence that God loves you as much as He loves Jesus Christ Himself. When you doubt the Father's love, you are straying from the faith.

Oh the power that is released when we believe and accept His love for us! He loves you despite your immaturity. He loves you even with your volatile temper problem. He loves you even with your body weight. He loves you even with your struggles with lust. He accepts you even with all your quirky ways. He accepts you because of who He is, not because of who you are. **Let the Holy Spirit place this deep within your consciousness: you are wildly and irrevocably loved and enjoyed by God!**

Allow these assurances of God's acceptance once again to wash your soul and renew your mind:

- "Yes, I have loved you with an everlasting love; therefore with lovingkindness I have drawn you" (Jeremiah 31:3).
- "the one who comes to Me I will by no means cast out" (John 6:37).
- to the praise of the glory of His grace, by which He has made us accepted in the Beloved (Ephesians 1:6).
- For you did not receive the spirit of bondage again to fear, but you received the Spirit of adoption by whom we cry out, "Abba, Father." The Spirit Himself bears witness with our spirit that we are children of God, and if children, then heirs—heirs of God and joint heirs with Christ, if indeed we suffer with Him, that we may also be glorified together (Romans 8:15-17).
- Therefore receive one another, just as Christ also received us, to the glory of God (Romans 15:7).

For some of you, this section is the key to your healing. **Until you are established on the inside in the love of God, you will always be susceptible to rejection's woundings.** Those who have not learned to find their satisfaction in the Father's acceptance always end up looking for it in all the wrong places. And instead of finding the acceptance they long for, they get rejected all over again. The only place of everlasting acceptance is in the arms of your loving Savior!

Holy Spirit, I pray that you would quicken these Scriptures to our hearts again today, that we might have power in our inner being to comprehend and know this love, and that the power of this love might heal the scars of any and every rejection we've known at the hand of man. Amen.

Chapter 5

Your Source Of Acceptance

Jesus Plus Nothing

The third step to healing from rejection is found in this simple but profound statement: **When God accepts me, I need acceptance from no one else.**

Now, it's *nice* to get acceptance from other people. But for the believer it's not *necessary*. When we realize we are accepted and embraced by the great God of the universe, the acceptance of people becomes secondary. All I really need is His acceptance. When I have that, I can face rejection from anyone and everyone else.

This is how Jesus lived. He had the Father's acceptance satisfying His soul on the inside, so He didn't need anyone else's acceptance to give Him a sense of self-identity. When the Father said, "this is My beloved Son in whom I am well pleased," I can imagine Jesus' heart response being something like, "That's all I need! Just to know You approve of My life, Father, is enough for Me. Now I am complete and at rest in Your affection and approval. I don't care who rejects Me, as long as I know You accept Me!"

If the Father is approving of our lives, the world can line up against us, throw rotten tomatoes at us, and call us nasty names — but it won't wound us on the inside because on the inside we are feeding on the Father's affirmation.

These were the implications behind this statement about Jesus: "But Jesus did not commit Himself to them, because He knew all men, and had no need that anyone should testify of man, for He knew what was in man" (John 2:24-25). Jesus knew he could not depend upon the acceptance of man, for men are fickle in their fallenness. The only acceptance that Jesus allowed to feed His spirit was the acceptance of the Father.

Somebody might say, "I know we're supposed to be satisfied with nothing but God's approval, but sometimes I just need a hug from some flesh and blood." I must disagree. As long as we look to flesh and blood for our approval, we will be snared by seasons of frustration and disappointment. I cannot back down on this point. My message is very direct: *Jesus plus nothing.* I need Jesus plus nothing else. When I have Him, I truly need nothing else. When I have His endorsement, I need no one else's endorsement. When I have His acceptance and approval, I need acceptance and approval from no other source. His acceptance alone is enough. I will build further upon this premise, so I cannot back down from it.

A Word Of Balance

Before moving on, however, I want to clarify what I *don't* mean. I want it to be clear that I am not advocating an independent spirit. I am *not* suggesting that we should have an attitude toward others that sounds like, "Hey buddy, Jesus endorses me, so scram."

The Lord has called us to walk in inter-dependence with our fellow believers in the body of Christ. We must not walk around as though we don't need the other members of the body in our life, because we desperately need each other! Jesus has constructed His kingdom in such a way that no one person gets the whole picture all the time. 1 Corinthians 12 articulates so beautifully the way each member of the body is dependent upon the other members of the body. So we all need each other in many, many ways.

We look to each other for encouragement, for counsel, for prayer support, for practical help, for wisdom, for perspective, for correction, etc. But we ought not look for others to be our source of acceptance. Our sense of acceptance comes from God alone.

This brings us to a very difficult and sensitive tension. On the one hand God calls us to relate to each other in humility, accountability, and mutual submission. The Scriptures exhort us to "be tender hearted" toward each other. But on the other hand, we are to be unmoved by man's rejection. So I am to open my heart to your love and correction, but I am to be unmoved and not wounded by your rejection. **I'm convinced this is one of the greatest challenges of Christian maturity: to make myself vulnerable to your kindness and affection, while not allowing myself to be penetrated by your rejection.**

When we close ourselves to the rejection of others, it's easy to close ourselves at the same time to their correction and rebuke. But each of us *needs* the corrective and loving rebukes of our brothers and sisters. So the tension here is very real, and the proper balance must be our constant pursuit.

It's a sign of maturity when we can receive correction without interpreting it as rejection.

What Is Your Source Of Acceptance?

Now I come to one of the most important principles of this book. This principle, properly understood and embraced, can be a tremendous catalyst for healing from the tyranny of rejection. Here it is:

You won't be healed of rejection by analyzing the source of your rejection but by looking at your source of acceptance.

Let me explain. Some people try to find healing from rejection's wounds by analyzing each instance in which they felt rejected. They go back and re-live painful experiences from their past and then ask God to bring healing to their hearts while they forgive those who wronged them.

The problem is simply this: it could take you days, weeks, or even months to analyze all your past rejections and deal with them in this methodical way. And then by the time you finish analyzing all your past rejections, it's taken you long enough that in the meantime you've accrued a whole new list of rejections. The list is never-ending. And then what about those rejections that you've overlooked?

No, I don't think that's the best way to be healed of rejection. I believe the healing comes, rather, in analyzing your source of acceptance. *To whom are you looking as the source of your acceptance?* This becomes the critical question.

We suffer rejection when we look for someone's acceptance but don't get it. Please re-read that statement carefully. Rejection is the result of looking for acceptance from man but not finding it. When we long for man's acceptance, we are setting ourselves up for rejection because other people are sinful and imperfect in their responses toward us. **When I yearn for your acceptance, I open myself to your rejection.**

The key is found in deciding that Jesus is going to become your sole source of acceptance. When you get to the place where your soul craves nothing but the acceptance of Jesus, you will no longer be victimized by the rejection of man.

Let's illustrate this truth with our former scenario—the earthly father who has rejected us all our life. Many of us are deeply wounded because we could never seem to meet our father's expectations, no matter how hard we tried. We battled for his acceptance, but instead got only rejection upon rejection.

So we decided to forgive our father. We allowed the grace of Jesus to wash and heal our past wounds. We felt free. But then something happened. We went home for Christmas. And while we were with our parents over the holiday season, our father exploded in a fit a rage like he's done for so many years. Every wound from the past seemed to get ripped open all over again, and we found ourselves crushed and rejected by our father all over again. **We had dealt with the wounds of the past but weren't equipped to handle the woundings of the present.**

Here's the question I want you to ask yourself: "To whom am I looking for approval and acceptance?" Is it possible that you are still searching, in some small way, for your earthly father's approval? If your soul is still groping in a small way for your father's acceptance, you are opening yourself to possible rejection and repetitive wounding. You desire his acceptance but never seem to get it the way you want it. Instead, you come away feeling rejected over and over.

When we hope for man's acceptance, we make ourselves vulnerable to man's rejection. I encourage you to decide today, "Lord, Your acceptance in my life is all I need. When You accept me, I need acceptance from no one else. I am complete in Your love."

Decide that from now on you are going to look for acceptance from none other than your heavenly Father. Let His acceptance fill and satisfy your heart. You no longer need your earthly father's acceptance because you are totally nurtured and completely satisfied by your heavenly Father's acceptance. "And you are complete in Him" (Colossians 2:10).

When you are complete in your heavenly Father's acceptance, and no longer crave your earthly father's acceptance, your father's rejection will no longer wound you. It will sting, but the Father's affections that you carry on the inside will quickly heal that pinprick of human rejection, granting you the grace to relate to your human father with love and forgiveness.

Closing The Door To Rejection

I said earlier in this book that the issues related to dealing with man's rejection and dealing with man's praise are identical. Here's where we see it. The issue is, are you seeking the acceptance of man? Those who want man's acceptance but don't get it succumb to feelings of rejection; those who want man's acceptance and get it fall into the snare of man's praise.

As long as you're seeking the acceptance of man, you are making yourself vulnerable to the rejection of man. **If man's acceptance will build you up, man's rejection will devastate you**. However, when you close yourself to needing the acceptance of man, you close the door to man's rejection.

This principle is reinforced in Ecclesiastes 7:21, "Also do not take to heart everything people say, lest you hear your servant cursing you."

Many people are touched by people's acceptance, and thus they are touched by their rejection. Their lives can become like an emotional roller coaster. Say something nice to them, and they're riding high; say something the wrong way to them, and they're devastated.

Jesus, in contrast, was absolutely steady in His emotional chemistry. **Jesus was not touched by the praise of man, so He was not wounded by the rejection of man**. And He got plenty of rejection!

I used to think Jesus was very thick-skinned. I saw Jesus as someone who was so tough that nothing could penetrate His soul and wound Him. But I had totally misunderstood who Jesus is. Jesus wasn't unmoved by rejection because He had a tough outer shell; He was untouched by rejection because He was untouched by acceptance. Man's rejections never penetrated His soul because He didn't allow man's praises to feed His soul.

Jesus found His complete identity in His Father's acceptance, and so can you and I! Again, to be fully satisfied in the Father's acceptance is not a hasty attainment, but a slow and growing process.

To repeat, we close the door to receiving man's rejection by closing the door to receiving man's acceptance and praise. When we're no longer inflated by others' acceptance, we'll no longer be deflated by their rejection.

We Can't Serve Two Masters

You cannot look for acceptance from both God and man. Follow this progression of thought carefully: When you seek someone's acceptance, you will try to please him. Whomever you desire to please, you become his servant. And, "'No one can serve two masters'" (Matthew 6:24).

You cannot serve both God and man. You cannot please both God and man. You cannot seek the acceptance of both God and man.

You must decide. Are you trying to please God or man? As we continue in this book, ask yourself these questions:

- Do I seek acceptance from man?
- When people compliment me, does it strengthen my sense of self-worth and self-fulfillment?
- Do I feed off the praise of man?

Chapter **6**

The Snare of
Man's Praise

So now we come to this great issue, the matter of the praise of man. Before we're through, I hope you'll see how the issues related to the rejection of man and the praise of man are very similar. Rejection and praise are opposite ends of the same continuum, with identical root issues.

The Scriptures are quite clear; we are not to actively seek out the praise of man. Jesus said, "'How can you believe, who receive honor from one another, and do not seek the honor that comes from the only God?'" (John 5:44). And after Jesus had taught the people, the Bible notes this about their response: "Nevertheless even among the rulers many believed in Him, but because of the Pharisees they did not confess Him, lest they should be put out of the synagogue, for they loved the praise of men more than the praise of God" (John 12:42-42).

Jesus denounced the religious leaders of His day because they were driven by the need to garner man's approval. So Jesus said, "'Beware of the scribes, who desire to go around in long robes, love greetings in the marketplaces, the best seats in the synagogues, and the best places at feasts'" (Luke 20:46). He also said of them, "'But all their works they do to be seen by men'" (Matthew 23:5). These passages are particularly stinging to me because of the natural desire in my flesh to be noticed by men. For those who long to please our Savior, these words put us on full alert. Clearly we are to seek the praise of God and not the praise of man.

Peter made two statements that are related to this subject:

"Whether it is right in the sight of God to listen to you more than to God, you judge" (Acts 4:19).

"We ought to obey God rather than men" (Acts 5:29).

Paul wrote, "For do I now persuade men, or God? Or do I seek to please men? For if I still pleased men, I would not be a bondservant of Christ" (Galatians 1:10). Paul also wrote this to the believers at Thessalonica:

But as we have been approved by God to be entrusted with the gospel, even so we speak, not as pleasing men, but God who tests our hearts. For neither at any time did we use flattering words, as you know, nor a cloak for covetousness—God is witness. Nor did we seek glory from men, either from you or from others, when we might have made demands as apostles of Christ (1 Thessalonians 2:4-6).

We should imitate the example of the apostle Paul who did not seek to please men but to please God alone. Indeed, Paul testified of the truly spiritual man that his "praise is not from men but from God" (Romans 2:29). The only praise we long to hear is from our Lord on the last day, "'Well done, good and faithful servant'" (Matthew 25:23).

Seeking the pleasure of God is in itself an all-consuming pursuit, without the additional burden of seeking to please people! I have been living recently in a very strong awareness of the reality of the fire that will touch our lives in the day of judgment:

Now if anyone builds on this foundation with gold, silver, precious stones, wood, hay, straw, each one's work will become clear; for the Day will declare it, because it will be revealed by fire; and the fire will test each one's work, of what sort it is. If anyone's work which he has built on it endures, he will receive a reward. If anyone's work is burned, he will suffer loss; but he himself will be saved, yet so as through fire (1 Corinthians 3:12-15).

This passage refers to the fire that will touch every believer's life in the day of judgment, testing the nature of our work in the kingdom. This passage tells me that the hard labors of many saints will disappear in the testing fire because they will be discovered to be "wood, hay, straw." The question is, *what kinds of labor in the kingdom constitute wood, hay, and straw?* The answer to that question is very complex, but one answer is this: *works that were accomplished out of a motive of pleasing man, to gain the attention and praise of man.* When the subtle desire for man's praise discolors our motives, the entire work is burned up! Therefore, this subject is of vast relevance to us who yearn for eternal rewards that will survive the testing fires of judgment.

In a very practical way, let's look at two reasons why we should not seek the praise of man.

People Are Undependable

There are two solid reasons why we should not be touched by the praise of man. Reason number one: **People are undependable.**

This is the people crying out "Hosanna!" to Christ at His triumphal entry into Jerusalem, and then one week later crying out, "Crucify Him!" Jesus knew He couldn't give Himself to their praises because in a few days their praises would turn to accusations.

If you seek the praise of men, they'll praise you today and prosecute you tomorrow. The hymnwriter was right, "The arm of flesh will fail you."

Even Christians are undependable. I've learned something about myself: if you'll get close enough to me for long enough, I'll eventually disappoint you. Because even though

I'm redeemed, I'm still human. This kind of disappointment from other Christians is something for which many are unprepared when they come to Christ. They are idealistic about what it means to be part of God's family. But as in every family, there are failures (in this life) between members of God's family. Prepare yourself now: *you will most certainly experience rejection in the body of Christ*. Accept the fact that it will be part of your life until Jesus returns.

Many people have even received rejection from me as I have attempted to minister to them and pastor them. In some cases, I handled them poorly; in some cases, they were set up in their own minds to receive rejection with just the slightest slip of the tongue. I never meant to reject them, but because of both my and their weakness and brokenness and limitations, they received my faltering attempts to love and serve them as rejection. (Some people will find rejection even where none was intended.) There have even been times when I thought I was showering someone with particular acceptance, only to later discover that they received my gestures as yet additional rejection. My point is, **even Christian leaders with their best and most sincere efforts are undependable.**

A common mistake among counselors today is to try to garner the trust of their counselees. I've heard counselors say, "I'm establishing a relationship with this person so that she will begin to trust me." The logic is that some people have been so rejected by others that they can't trust anyone, and until they are able to trust their counselor they will not be able to receive from their counselor. But when counselors try to get someone to trust them, they are steering them contrary to the guidance of Scripture: "Do not put your trust in princes, nor in a son of man, in whom there is no help. His spirit departs, he returns to his earth; in that very day his plans perish" (Psalm 146:3-4). ("Princes" represent ministry leaders, those who are responsible for providing spiritual direction for others.) Those who put their trust in man will always be disappointed. Either man will fail you in your time of need, or he will do something to scandalize you, or he will move away from you, or even under the best of circumstances (supposing that the man of God is faithful and true throughout his entire lifetime), he will die on you. So now the one upon whom you've come to trust and depend is dead! I've heard of people who were angry at funerals, angry at the person for dying. It's because they had put their trust in that person, and now that person had "up and died" on them! Our duty is to trust but one: God. We are to love one another and be faithful to one another, but to trust God alone.

You can't put your trust in any human! Every human being will fail you, given enough time. There is only one whom you can trust—your Father in heaven.

So when your fellow man praises you, don't let it sway your heart. The one who praises you today may very possibly disappoint you tomorrow.

People's Opinions Are Insignificant

The second reason we should not be warmed by the praise of man is this: **The opinions of people are insignificant.**

What other people think about you really doesn't matter—at all. When you stand before God's throne, their opinion of your life will be irrelevant. In fact, even your own opinion of your life will be irrelevant. "For not he who commends himself is approved, but whom the Lord commends" (2 Corinthians 10:18).

At that moment before God's throne, there will be only one opinion in the universe that will matter—God's! "Therefore judge nothing before the time, until the Lord comes, who will both bring to light the hidden things of darkness and reveal the counsels of the hearts. Then each one's praise will come from God" (1 Corinthians 4:5).

We tend to view some people as more significant than others. For example, we tend to view prominent Christian leaders as carrying more weight in the kingdom than others. If someone knows Pat Robertson personally and knows that Pat enjoys him as a person, he might allow that relationship to make him feel better about himself. But the psalmist wrote, "Surely men of low degree are a vapor, men of high degree are a lie; if they are weighed on the scales, they are altogether lighter than vapor" (Psalm 62:9).

So put together your "who's who" list of whom you might consider to be "men of high degree." You might come up with names like Billy Graham, Jack Hayford, Max Lucado, Bill Bright, Bill Hybels, Mother Teresa, Chuck Smith, James Dobson, Joyce Meier, or others. Put all those you consider "spiritual heavyweights" on spiritual scales, and the psalmist says their compounded weight is "altogether lighter than vapor." In other words, not only do they weigh nothing, they weigh less than nothing. **Like helium, which rises because it is lighter than air, the opinions of men—the most important men you can think of—are lighter than vapor.**

So when someone gives you a compliment, consider the source. Consider that the praise is coming from less-than-vapor.

When someone says, "My, you look good today," you're thinking to yourself, "Thanks for the vaporous remark." On the outside you're polite, of course, and reply with a gracious, "Thank you." But on the inside you're not receiving the praise.

Someone gives you a sincere compliment: "That was a wonderful thought you shared tonight in our cell group! I've never thought of it like that before! You certainly have a remarkable way of making deep Scriptural truths easy to understand."

And you're thinking, "Vapor!"

The praises of people are not only insignificant, they are a negative reading on the significance chart. But when your heavenly Father honors you, now *there's* something significant! **We should live for but one thing: the praise of God.** Anything else is insignificant.

Paul's Sensitivity

The desire for the praise and approval of man runs very deep in our sinful flesh. We can crucify the desire for man's praise, but it keeps resurfacing in our flesh in all kinds of creative and fresh ways.

Paul was aware of the insidious trap that young men fall into, for they can easily convince themselves that their motives are totally pure in seeking the praise of God alone, when in fact this desire for the praise of man is still a very strong issue within them. Paul showed his sensitivity to this issue in the way he related to one brother in the book of Second Corinthians.

Here's the context of the matter to which I refer:

"But thanks be to God who puts the same earnest care for you into the heart of Titus. For he not only accepted the exhortation, but being more diligent, he went to you of his own accord. And we have sent with him the brother whose praise is in the gospel throughout all the churches, and not only that, but who was also chosen by the churches to travel with us with this gift, which is administered by us to the glory of the Lord Himself and to show your ready mind, avoiding this: that anyone should blame us in this lavish gift which is administered by us—providing honorable things, not only in the sight of the Lord, but also in the sight of men. And we have sent with them our brother whom we have often proved diligent in many things, but now much more diligent, because of the great confidence which we have in you. If anyone inquires about Titus, he is my partner and fellow worker concerning you. Or if our brethren are inquired about, they are messengers of the churches, the glory of Christ" (2 Corinthians 8:16-23).

Paul is writing about two brothers—Titus and an unnamed brother. Titus is mentioned twice by name and commended; the other brother is left nameless. Why does Paul not mention the other brother's name? Because Paul knew the power of name recognition.

There's something intoxicating about seeing your name in print and having your name known by others. I've tasted of that wine personally just a little bit; Paul also knew all about that. And he was aware that the brother to which he was referring didn't have the maturity to handle the fame properly. So Paul refused to make his name known. There's no doubt in my mind that the unnamed brother was young, new in ministry, and still in training. Titus, on the other hand, was safe to name because of his evident maturity and proven faithfulness.

We might almost think this was an accidental oversight on Paul's part until we realize that he repeated the same thing the second time in the same epistle. The following verse comes four chapters later:

I urged Titus, and sent our brother with him. Did Titus take advantage of you? Did we not walk in the same spirit? Did we not walk in the same steps? (2 Corinthians 12:18).

For the second time, Paul mentioned Titus twice by name while leaving his companion nameless.

For the time being, the brother was to remain an unknown. This would not only save him from the seduction of fame, it would also refine him through Paul's obvious refusal to mention his name. I can imagine him thinking, "He mentions Titus twice, but doesn't mention my name even once! In two portions of the same letter! What is Paul's point? Does he think I have a problem? Furthermore, why is this bothering me so much? I can't believe I'm bugged by something so trivial!" Paul was being used by the Holy Spirit to help the brother deal with a very important issue in his life—the same thing that all of us have to deal with. The desire for name recognition. It's the praise of man, and it's inebriating.

The Snare Of Man's Praise

Magrate Yap once said to me, "The root of anger is the fear of rejection." She was talking about an eruptive kind of anger that many people battle. The reason some people have an habitual struggle with eruptive anger, Magrate said, is that they fear rejection. **Those who fear the rejection of man have a deep yearning for the praise of man and set their souls up for repetitive heartache.** Their response to that pain is expressed in anger. That's why the Scriptures say, "The fear of man brings a snare" (Proverbs 29:25).

The fear of man snares, but the fear of God frees. When we open ourselves to being concerned about man's opinion of our lives, we're making ourselves vulnerable to a snare.

This is what happened to Joshua and the elders of Israel. Joshua was the new leader of Israel, and by the Lord's help he had led the people to two great victories—over the Canaanite cities of Jericho and Ai. Both cities were conquered and destroyed, and the reputation of Israel's battle prowess was spreading like wildfire throughout the land. So the people of Gibeon, a Canaanite city, put their heads together and came up with a plan to save their necks. They wanted to formulate a treaty with Joshua, so they came to him in costume, pretending to be from a very distant land. When Joshua asked the delegation from Gibeon where they were from, they replied:

> *"From a very far country your servants have come, because of the name of the LORD your God; for we have heard of His fame, and all that He did in Egypt, and all that He did to the two kings of the Amorites who were beyond the Jordan—to Sihon king of Heshbon, and Og king of Bashan, who was at Ashtaroth. Therefore our elders and all the inhabitants of our country spoke to us, saying, 'Take provisions with you for the journey, and go to meet them, and say to them, "We are your servants; now therefore, make a covenant with us."' This bread of ours we took hot for our provision from our houses on the day we departed to come to you. But now look, it is dry and moldy. And these wineskins which we filled were new, and see, they are torn; and these our garments and our sandals have become old because of the very long journey." Then the men of Israel took some of their provisions; but they did not ask counsel of the LORD. So Joshua made peace with them, and made a covenant with them to let them live; and the rulers of the congregation swore to them* (Joshua 9:9-15).

Notice that the delegation from Gibeon started their whole spiel with a litany of praises. Their tactic worked because Joshua and the rulers were touched by the honor of these men. Hearing that their reputation had gone far and wide, the leaders of Israel were flattered and began to feel a false sense of self-satisfaction. They lowered their guard and were snared into a treaty by a Canaanite city.

The Jewish leaders of Jesus' day were also snared by their desire for man's praises (which is the fear of man). When Jesus asked them if John's baptism was from heaven or from men, they were not able to give Him a straight answer because "they feared the people, for all counted John to have been a prophet indeed" (Mark 11:32). It's a sad day when spiritual leaders are governed by the fear of man. "The fear of man brings a snare, but whoever trusts in the LORD shall be safe" (Proverbs 29:25). **The one you fear is the one you will seek to please**.

It was the Pharisee's love of man's praise that froze their ability to move with God. "Nevertheless even among the rulers many believed in Him, but because of the Pharisees they did not confess Him, lest they should be put out of the synagogue; for they loved the praise of men more than the praise of God" (John 12:42-43).

Herod was also snared by man's praise. The people of Tyre and Sidon, in trying to curry Herod's favor, kept on responding to his oration with shouts of, "'The voice of a god and not of a man!'" (Acts 12:22). And because Herod "did not give glory to God," he was "eaten by worms and died." The praise of man will kill you from the inside out. Bob Mumford put it this way: **"Praise is food for God, poison for man."**

Billy Graham once said, "You're never more like the devil than when you want credit for what you do." The praise of man is a snare.

Chapter 7

Jesus and the Praise of Man

Jesus And Flattery

Jesus was not moved by the praise of man. I see this truth at the triumphal entry when the children were singing and twirling and dancing. They were lavishing Jesus with some very warm and sincere praises. If the praise of man were ever to touch His heart, surely it would be the praises of these delightful, innocent children. But just as the praise service started to gain some real momentum, Jesus began to weep (see Luke 19:41). They were praising, but Jesus was weeping!

This tells me that Jesus lived totally independent of their praises. If I were Jesus on this occasion, my flesh would have been touched by this praise. I would have been riding high on that donkey: "You know it! That's right! Come on, now, let the praises arise! Let it go!"

But instead of being captured by their accolades, Jesus is unmoved. He's walking to the beat of an internal drummer. His heart begins to break over the city of Jerusalem, just as they're gearing the praise service into an even higher level. And He begins to weep with the Father's heartbreak over the people who did not receive Him.

If His heart had been warmed by their praises, He would have never been able to discern the Father's heart for the city.

I'd like to point to one more incident which reveals how Jesus responded to the praises of men. Here's our passage:

> *Then they sent to Him some of the Pharisees and the Herodians, to catch Him in His words. When they had come, they said to Him, "Teacher, we know that You are true, and care about no one; for You do not regard the person of men, but teach the way of God in truth. Is it lawful to pay taxes to Caesar, or not? Shall we pay, or shall we not pay?" But He, knowing their hypocrisy, said to them, "Why do you test Me? Bring Me a denarius that I may see it." So they brought it. And He said to them, "Whose image and inscription is this?" They said to Him, "Caesar's." And Jesus answered and said to them, "Render to Caesar the things that are Caesar's, and to God the things that are God's." And they marveled at Him* (Mark 12:13-17).

These leaders were laying a trap for him. They supposed if they "buttered up" Jesus with flattery and praise that He would be warmed by the compliments, drop His guard, and make a slip with His tongue. But since He wasn't touched by their praise, He was able to see their hypocrisy.

When we're energized by men's praises, we lose our discernment. We lose our ability to discern the Father's agenda, and we lose the ability to discern the duplicitous motives of man. Since Jesus wasn't entangled by man's praise, He was free to remain sensitive to the Father's heart and agenda, and He was able to discern their surreptitious trap.

This same trap seeks to ensnare those who have been granted higher levels of anointing by the Holy Spirit. With the greater anointing comes the greater praise of man. This syndrome is an absolute guarantee: when God anoints you in an unusual way beyond that of your companions, the people of God will express their gratitude and honor to you with great sincerity and enthusiasm. They think they're encouraging you, but they're actually presenting you with a great test. Will you take in their praises? Will you believe their words? Will you start to view yourself through their eyes? Will you believe your own press?

It's very difficult, when you are bombarded over and over by grateful saints who have benefited from your ministry, to keep your head clear from their praises. It's precisely for this reason that God so often withholds the greater anointings. Unless you have been crushed in the school of the Spirit, you will not be sensitized to the treacherous nature of this trap. **Without the crushing, the higher anointings will cause you to self-destruct.** You'll start to enjoy the praises—and you'll lose your discernment. Once you forfeit that cutting-edge discernment, you will eventually play the fool.

The Inward Voice Of Affirmation

Jesus evaluated His ministry, not based upon the praise of man, but based upon the inner witness of the Holy Spirit. Jesus' example tells us: you don't need a message written in the sky, telling you how wonderful you are. You don't need a vision or dream upon your bed, endorsing your actions. All you need is that inner voice of the Spirit.

On one occasion, the Father validated Jesus' ministry with a thunderous voice from the sky, and Jesus' response is most intriguing:

> *"Now My soul is troubled, and what shall I say? 'Father, save Me from this hour'? But for this purpose I came to this hour. Father, glorify Your name." Then a voice came from heaven, saying, "I have both glorified it and will glorify it again." Therefore the people who stood by and heard it said that it had thundered. Others said, "An angel has spoken to Him." Jesus answered and said, "This voice did not come because of Me, but for your sake"* (John 12:27-30).

If, while I was preaching, God Himself thundered from the heavens in the English language to my listeners, I can only imagine what my response might be. I would probably

be tempted to think, "Don't you guys get it? God is affirming Me from heaven! Don't you see that I'm God's chosen
one? Can't you understand that God's imprimatur is on my
ministry?" My confidence level would probably quadruple
if God thundered His endorsement of my ministry from the
sky.

But that wasn't how Jesus responded at all. He said, "This
voice did not come because of Me." Basically He was saying, "This voice from heaven adds nothing to My life. This
voice didn't come in order to make Me feel better about
Myself. I am not moved even by a thunderous voice in the
heavens. I don't need a supernatural manifestation to know
that the Father affirms Me." I can suppose Jesus adding, "All
I need is that inner witness of the Holy Spirit."

In the weakness of my flesh, my human tendency is to
desire for God to endorse me in a spectacular way. But such
manifestations are not to be our source of affirmation. The
only affirmation we should ever need is that inner voice of
the Father, "You are my beloved child, in you I am well
pleased."

Receiving Honor From Men

Jesus stated His position on this subject with absolute clarity: "I do not receive honor from men" (John 5:41).

He didn't simply say, "I don't go around seeking the
honor of men." He said something much stronger: "When
the compliments come, I don't even receive them."

When someone would pay Him a compliment for His
teaching or miracle ministry, Jesus would respond on the
inside, "I don't receive that." The only honor Jesus received
was that of His Father.

Jesus then went on to say, "'How can you believe, who
receive honor from one another, and do not seek the honor
that comes from the only God?'" (John 5:44). It's as though
Jesus were saying, "I don't understand you people. Why do
you settle for something so paltry as the honor that man can
give, when there is something so far greater available to you?

The honor of man is so insignificant in contrast to the riches of the extravagant honor that your Heavenly Father is able to bestow!"

"Looking unto Jesus, the author and finisher of our faith, who for the joy that was set before Him endured the cross, despising the shame" (Hebrews 12:2). What was this joy that was set before Him? More than anything else, I believe Jesus was referring to the explosive, superabundant honor the Father would profusely lavish upon Him in glory.

I can imagine the Father, sometime in the ages past, saying something like this to the Son: "Son, if You will embrace the suffering and death of the cross, it will please My heart greatly, and I will honor You."

And I can imagine the Son replying, "O holy Father, there are only two things I live for—to please You, and to receive Your honor. I would do anything for that!"

Jesus understood what it meant to be honored by the Father, and so it was for this that He lived and died. And did the Father honor Him? Oh my, how He honored Him! "Therefore God also has highly exalted Him and given Him the name which is above every name, that at the name of Jesus every knee should bow, of those in heaven, and of those on earth, and of those under the earth, and that every tongue should confess that Jesus Christ is Lord, to the glory of God the Father" (Philippians 2:9-11).

Hold out, dear friend, for the highest honor! Don't receive the cheap replacement of man's praise when you can contend for the highest praise—the honor of God Himself.

Chapter 8

How Daniel Handled the Praise of Man

Daniel is a man who found victory in his soul in this area of receiving the praise of man. His example is inspiring and instructive. He models for us what it means to seek God's honor even when men would lavish their honor upon us.

Greatly Beloved

Twice Daniel is told by a heavenly messenger that he is "greatly beloved" by God:

> *And he said to me, "O Daniel, man greatly beloved, understand the words that I speak to you, and stand upright, for I have now been sent to you"* (Daniel 10:11).

> *And he said, "O man greatly beloved, fear not! Peace be to you; be strong, yes, be strong!" So when he spoke to me I was strengthened, and said, "Let my lord speak, for you have strengthened me"* (Daniel 10:19).

This heavenly messenger is emphasizing to Daniel, "Daniel, God *really* has a thing for you. Of all the men on earth, you are the recipient of an unusual and most profound affection. God has such a special love for you that He has sent me to give you a singularly outstanding vision and revelation." And sure enough, Daniel was given such awesome heavenly visions that he couldn't even stand up. The wonder of what he saw is exceeded in Scripture only by the revelation of Jesus Christ that was given to the apostle John (the Book of Revelation).

So I find myself asking, "What did Daniel do to incur this kind of affection from God? Why did God like him so much?" When I looked at it carefully, I came away with the personal conviction that it was because Daniel lived only for the honor of God and was totally indifferent toward the honor that man gives.

The story that reveals this quality in Daniel is written in the fifth chapter of his book.

Daniel 5

Daniel 5:1 Belshazzar the king made a great feast for a thousand of his lords, and drank wine in the presence of the thousand. 2 While he tasted the wine, Belshazzar gave the command to bring the gold and silver vessels which his father Nebuchadnezzar had taken from the temple which had been in Jerusalem, that the king and his lords, his wives, and his concubines might drink from them. 3 Then they brought the gold vessels that had been taken from the temple of the house of God which had been in Jerusalem; and the king and his lords, his wives, and his concubines drank from them. 4 They drank wine, and praised the gods of gold and silver, bronze and iron, wood and stone. 5 In the same hour the fingers of a man's hand appeared and wrote opposite the lampstand on the plaster of the wall of the king's palace; and the king saw the part of the hand that wrote. 6 Then the king's countenance changed, and his thoughts troubled him, so that the joints of his hips were loosened and his knees knocked against each other. 7 The king cried aloud to bring in the astrologers, the Chaldeans, and the soothsayers. The king spoke, saying to the wise men of Babylon, "Whoever reads this writing, and tells me its interpretation, shall be clothed with purple and have a chain of gold around his neck; and he shall be the third ruler in the kingdom." 8 Now all the king's wise men came, but they could not read the writing, or make known to the king its interpretation. 9 Then King Belshazzar was greatly troubled, his countenance was changed, and his lords were astonished. 10 The queen, because of the words of the king and his lords, came to the banquet hall. The queen spoke, saying, "O king, live forever! Do not let your thoughts trouble you, nor let your countenance change. 11 There is a man in your kingdom in whom is the Spirit of the Holy God. And in the days of your father, light and understanding and wisdom, like the wisdom of the gods, were found in him; and King Nebuchadnezzar your father—your father the king—made him chief of the magicians, astrologers, Chaldeans, and soothsayers. 12 Inasmuch as an excellent spirit, knowledge, understanding, interpreting dreams, solving riddles, and explaining enigmas were found in this Daniel, whom the king named Belteshazzar, now let Daniel be called, and he will give the interpretation." 13 Then Daniel was brought in before the king. The king spoke, and said to Daniel, "Are you that Daniel who is one of the captives from Judah, whom my father the king brought from Judah? 14 I have heard of you, that the Spirit of God is in you, and that light and understanding and excellent wisdom are found in you. 15 Now the wise men, the astrologers, have been brought in before me, that they should read this writing and make known to me its interpretation, but they could not give the interpretation of the thing. 16 And I have heard of you, that you can give interpretations and explain enigmas. Now if you can read the writing and make known to me its interpretation, you shall be clothed with purple and have a chain of gold around your neck, and shall be the third ruler in the kingdom." 17 Then Daniel answered, and said before the king, "Let your gifts be for yourself, and give your rewards to another; yet I will read the writing to the king, and make known to him the interpretation. 18 O king, the Most High God gave Nebuchadnezzar your father a kingdom and majesty, glory and honor. 19 And because of the majesty that He gave

*him, all peoples, nations, and languages trembled and feared
before him. Whomever he wished, he executed; whomever
he wished, he kept alive; whomever he wished, he set up;
and whomever he wished, he put down. 20 But when his
heart was lifted up, and his spirit was hardened in pride,
he was deposed from his kingly throne, and they took his
glory from him. 21 Then he was driven from the sons of
men, his heart was made like the beasts, and his dwelling
was with the wild donkeys. They fed him with grass like
oxen, and his body was wet with the dew of heaven, till he
knew that the Most High God rules in the kingdom of men,
and appoints over it whomever He chooses. 22 But you his
son, Belshazzar, have not humbled your heart, although
you knew all this. 23 And you have lifted yourself up
against the Lord of heaven. They have brought the vessels
of His house before you, and you and your lords, your wives
and your concubines, have drunk wine from them. And
you have praised the gods of silver and gold, bronze and
iron, wood and stone, which do not see or hear or know;
and the God who holds your breath in His hand and owns
all your ways, you have not glorified. 24 Then the fingers
of the hand were sent from Him, and this writing was written. 25 And this is the inscription that was written: MENE,
MENE, TEKEL, UPHARSIN. 26 This is the interpretation of each word. MENE: God has numbered your kingdom, and finished it; 27 TEKEL: You have been weighed
in the balances, and found wanting; 28 PERES: Your kingdom has been divided, and given to the Medes and Per-
sians." 29 Then Belshazzar gave the command, and they
clothed Daniel with purple and put a chain of gold around
his neck, and made a proclamation concerning him that he
should be the third ruler in the kingdom.*

Writing On The Wall

This passage describes a gala party in Babylon. While
the wine is flowing, the food is bountiful, and the festivities
are in full swing, suddenly a hand appears out of nowhere

and writes something cryptic on the wall. Nobody in Belshazzar's kingdom is able to read and interpret the handwriting.

Then the Queen Mother enters the ballroom to speak to her son. She remembers how Daniel had interpreted the dreams of her late husband, king Nebuchadnezzar. So she says to the king, "You ought to find Daniel. He would be able to read and interpret the handwriting."

Belshazzar immediately fetches Daniel. Now, Daniel is not to be found in his former residence. At one time, he had served as Nebuchadnezzar's right hand man and so would have lived near the king's palace. But when Belshazzar became king, he dismissed the cabinet members that had served his father and appointed his own cabinet. Daniel was ousted from his prestigious place of responsibility and influence at the king's right hand. Daniel 8:27 indicates that Daniel still worked for King Belshazzar, but it was in a much more menial and insignificant position. Daniel had been demoted, so they search to see where he now lives, and they find him.

Flattery And Praise

When they bring Daniel before Belshazzar, the first thing Belshazzar does is flatter him. Twice he says to Daniel, "I have heard of you" (verses 14 & 16). For a man who has been demoted to a menial job in some corner somewhere, these words of praise must have pulled at Daniel's ego. Imagine the President of the United States calling you into his Oval Office and saying to you, "I have heard of you." Now that would be impressive! Here is Belshazzar, the most powerful man in the world, acknowledging that Daniel's reputation has gone before him. "You're the talk of the king's court." That's very flattering indeed.

Then Belshazzar offers to reinstate Daniel to his former position, provided that he is able to read and interpret the handwriting on the wall. Keep in mind that Daniel has been sent out to pasture. He's a discarded nobody. He's a semi-retired "has been" whom everyone has forgotten. And suddenly he faces an opportunity to regain honor, prestige, power, position, and wealth. All the other court members are drooling at the offer that has just been extended to him. What will Daniel say?

Daniel's response is most amazing. The flattery doesn't inflate his ego. The king's honor doesn't seduce him. The possibility of prestigious advancement doesn't make his heart race. Instead, he retorts to the king, "'Let your gifts be for yourself, and give your rewards to another; yet I will read the writing to the king, and make known to him the interpretation'" (verse 17). I want you to see that Daniel was completely unmoved by the king's compliments and honor. Far from tantalized, he is completely unimpressed with the honor that this mighty Monarch could bestow.

Living For God's Honor

If we could ask Daniel why the king's honor meant so little to him, I think he would tell us something like this: "Because there's only one thing I live for—the honor that God can bestow."

Daniel was a man who despised the honor that man could give because he valued the honor that God could give. And *this*, I believe, is one reason why God loved him so much. God is like, "Wow—this is incredible! I've got a man who values My honor so much that he repudiates the highest honors of man. I love this man! Here's a vessel that I can use."

I fully believe the reason the hand appeared and wrote on the wall, in the first place, was because God had a Daniel. If there had been no Daniel, there would have been no handwriting on the wall. God had a man who esteemed the honor of God over the honor of man, and so He was able to work in a most intriguing way to speak to the king of Babylon.

When God has a man (like Daniel) who is not touched by the praise of man, He is able to accelerate His purposes in the earth. These kinds of consecrated servants become dangerous vessels that God is able to use in profound and unique ways to accomplish His endtime strategies.

Chapter 9

The Critical Implications of Overcoming

The issues at stake in this subject are absolutely crucial in their significance. If we come to terms with the praise of man, we will be guided toward the path of true kingdom fruitfulness. If we lose it here, we hazard becoming casualties in the war that rages all about us. In this chapter, I want to articulate how important it is that we press into victory over the destructive tentacles of man's praise.

Release of Kingdom Authority

The first issue at stake is this: Will God find worthy vessels with which He can entrust the higher dimensions of kingdom authority which will be necessary to consummate the final ingathering and prepare the bride for the Bridegroom's return?

There is a great cry in the church today, "Lord, send Your power! Revive Your works; make them known in our generation. Lord, use us in the power manifestations of Your Holy Spirit!" This is a noble prayer that God longs to answer, but can He find vessels that will be safe conduits of that kind of power?

Here's the problem. When God entrusts the higher dimensions of kingdom authority to His chosen servants, the people of God fawn over them like they're spiritual superstars. That kind of praise can easily intoxicate God's servants, causing them to violate their stewardship of the power giftings without even realizing it.

This was one of the ramifications of Jesus' statement, "'How can you believe, who receive honor from one another, and do not seek the honor that comes from the only God?'" (John 5:44). Jesus was saying, "How can you believe—that is, how can I give you great miracle-working faith to believe for power manifestations—when you're so easily warmed by the honor of man?" Jesus was saying He could not give this kind of faith to those who feed off the praise of man. There is nothing more damaging to the kingdom than someone who has a little bit of power flowing through their lives, but who is touched by man's praises. Because when God starts to use you just a little bit in healing the sick or raising the dead, people will pour all kinds of attention on you. "For men will praise you when you do well for yourself" (Psalm 49:18). They will fuss, push, fawn, follow. They will interview you on their radio and TV stations, they will put your picture in their magazine, and they will make you feel incredibly important. This kind of attention is a guaranteed companion of power ministries, and when you begin to enjoy the attention, you are headed for turbulent waters.

If the fawning attention of man can find a place in your soul, you will self-destruct. So Jesus says, "I love you too much to give you that kind of faith and power." So He does a great pruning in our hearts, in order to cut away and remove that desire for the praise of man.

Jesus' miracles were the way the Father honored Him. That's what Jesus was pointing to when He said, "It is My Father who honors Me" (John 8:54). Here's the reason the Father honored Christ with this flow of miracle anointing: because Jesus' sole passion was to glorify the Father. Jesus' passion was not that He look good, but that the Father look good.

Mike Bickle has said that God isn't interested in making men, ministries, or churches famous. He's committed to spreading the fame of His Son throughout the nations. Amen! I believe God is reserving the greater power—the mightier release of His Spirit—for the time when the church seeks to proclaim the riches of Christ's marvelous personality (Ephesians 3:8). **He will anoint and empower believers who seek to capture the hearts of others for His Son, not for themselves.** The greater dimensions of faith will be given to those who are not touched by the praise of man. They will do great exploits because their only passion will be to further the reputation of the beautiful Son of God.

The I-Word

If we do not deal with this business of the praise of man, we succumb to the greatest of all offences. Let me explain.

Jesus wants to be everything to us. He wants to be our food, our drink, our sustenance, our life. He wants us to have no other gods before Him. He doesn't want us receiving life from anything but Him. To be energized by the honor of man is to find fulfillment in something which Jesus despised.

As I meditated upon this, here's what I saw: **To seek the honor of man is idolatry.**

Idolatry is a strong word, but what other word can be used for it? When I am feeding off something other than Christ, I have no other definition for that but idolatry. Jesus said, "My food is to do the will of the Father" (John 4:34). Doing the Father's will was Jesus' source of nourishment and delight. God wants to be my only sustenance. When I feed off the praise of man, I am finding my source in something other than Jesus. To find my source of life in something other than Jesus Christ is idolatry.

I am dealing right now with what may possibly be the greatest stronghold of idolatry in the lives of believers everywhere—being nourished by the approval and honor of man. It's not without reason that the apostle John appealed to the believers in his old age by closing his first epistle with these words, "Little children, keep yourselves from idols. Amen" (1 John 5:21).

> *O Lord, this form of idolatry was never the willful intention of our heart! We never meant to make the praises of man something that nourished us in an idolatrous way. We repent, Lord! Forgive us, and empower us to feed only on the honor that comes from doing the will of the only God.*

Accuracy Of Ministry

Again, the implications of dealing rightly with this area are so crucial to God's kingdom purposes. Let me go to another ramification of our subject matter—the question of ministry effectiveness.

The verse that has challenged me the most, in terms of my struggle with my flesh's desiring the praises of man, is John 7:18, "'He who speaks from himself seeks his own glory; but He who seeks the glory of the One who sent Him is true, and no unrighteousness is in Him.'" I have been so convicted by this Scripture because Jesus is saying that every time I speak something that originates in my heart I am seeking my own glory. Every time I preach a sermon that has not gotten its impetus from the heart of the Father, I am speaking out of my own resources and, thus, am seeking to look good before people. I'm subconsciously groping for their praise.

In contrast, Jesus goes on to say that the one who speaks the message that God has sovereignly given Him to speak is not trying to look good before people. His only concern is to look good in God's eyes, so his passion is to deliver God's message as faithfully as he possibly can.

Jesus says that such a one "is true." The word "true" is an archer's term. The one who speaks only what God has sent him to speak is like an arrow: he hits true to the mark. This is our passion in ministry, to hit "the bull's eye," the center of the target. But so often we find ourselves hitting somewhere close. We're not way off, but we're not hitting dead center either. The reason is, there is something in the crevasses of our flesh that is wanting for our listeners to be impressed with us. As a result, our ministry does not have its potential impact.

"But He who seeks the glory of the One who sent Him is true." Only the one who seeks to glorify God (really and truly) is able to be "true" to the mark. **When we carry even the slightest desire to impress those around us, arrows that we deploy in ministry may start out right, but then in transit they veer away from the mark.** It's because they're not deployed from a heart that is "true"—from a motive that seeks nothing but to honor the Son of God.

I am amazed at what Jesus says about the one who seeks the glory of the One who sent him. He said there is "no unrighteousness is in Him." What an incredible declaration! In other words, *if I can get to the place where the only motivation that fills my heart is to bring honor and glory to God, then I will have arrived at a place of sinlessness.*

In other words, Jesus is saying, "**This is the final frontier.** This is the last and great battlefield in bringing your soul into subjection. If you can successfully conquer this desire in your heart for the praise of man, you will have attained Christian perfection."

If only we could get to the place where there is no desire whatsoever within us to look good before men and an exclusive and burning desire to see God glorified! When we crucify this desire to find glory before men, we are dealing with the central core issue of being dead to self and alive to God. Once we have perfected that attainment we will truly have entered into the grace of Christian perfection. For this we strain.

> *O Lord, is this perhaps one reason why I've felt that my ministry has never reached its potential of impact? I repent, Lord, of wanting to impress people with my ministry giftings. May the only thing that motivates my heart be a passion to represent Your message truthfully and faithfully to Your people, regardless of their impression of me as the vessel. I call upon Your grace. Help me Lord!*

Free Of All Men

In this chapter, I've been giving reasons why it is imperative that we deal violently and conclusively with the way our hearts want to feel "warm fuzzies" from the praises of man. My final point is that this is the only way to enter fully into the liberty for which Christ died to give us, that we not be entangled again with any yoke of bondage (Galatians 5:1).

The Scriptures point out that when a man has something to lose, he lives under the duress of trying to protect what he owns (see Proverbs 13:8). When you're rich, you're susceptible to blackmail. But you can't blackmail a pauper because he has nothing to lose.

Those with no reputation have nothing to lose. Those who have a good reputation will seek to protect it. Those who seek to cultivate a good reputation become vulnerable to the praise of man. Jesus was free from man's praise because He made Himself of no reputation (Philippians 2:7). He had nothing to lose.

When I have nothing to lose, I'm free. I can't be bought, blackmailed, or coerced. I have no reputation to maintain, so I'm free from the praise of man.

When I'm in Christ I already have everything I need, so I have need of nothing. I no longer need honor from people. I already have all things, so I have nothing to gain. Jesus had no reputation so He had nothing to lose—and all that the Father had was His so He had nothing to gain. With nothing to lose or gain, He was free of all men. In the same way I have nothing to lose or gain, so I can be totally free of the snare of man's praise.

When I no longer receive the praise of man, I become free of all men. What I mean is, I become free to love all men equally and unconditionally. I can love everyone regardless of their attitude or action toward me.

When your praise doesn't touch me and your rejection doesn't wound me, I am a free agent. I am able to relate to you in total freedom, for nothing you do can control who I am and how I relate to you.

Jesus manifested this freedom in loving others. He knew His disciples would forsake and leave Him at His arrest, and He even prophesied that they would be thus scattered from Him. But even so, John testified of Jesus that just before His arrest, "Having loved His own who were in the world, He loved them to the end" (John 13:1). In others words, knowing they would reject Him, Jesus still showed them the fullness of His love right to the end.

This is the freedom I'm straining toward. Do you accept and honor me? I love you without showing you any favoritism.

Do you reject me? I love you anyways. I love you, if it were possible, with the same love with which Christ loves you. You can put nails in my hands and hang me on a tree, but my love for you does not change.

This is the freedom Jesus died to give us.

Chapter ***10***

God's Commitment to Help Us Overcome

So how do we gain victory over the deceptive magnetism of man's praise? Before I address that question, I want to emphasize that I personally don't live in fullness of victory, so I am not writing this as some kind of expert who has conquered this beast. In fact, if anything, I am in more pain today than ever over my own carnality in this area.

Truthfully, my flesh still craves affirmation. My flesh is much more interested in the opinions of the people I see than in the opinion of the One I don't see.

We pastors and teachers have our "creative ways" of fishing for compliments. After Sunday morning services, I would find a clever way to get my wife's opinion on my sermon, hoping of course that she would declare it the most profound message she has ever heard me utter. So I would say something like, "How did the preacher do today, Sweetheart?"

Then the Lord nailed me: "You're looking for the praise of your wife rather than of Me." So I did some real fast repenting! And I began to pray, "Lord, what was *Your* opinion of this preacher today?"

I've discovered it's possible to impress people with my ministry but not have the full pleasure of God. Just because I have the praise of man doesn't mean I've got the praise of God.

I noticed that Jesus had the habit of praying *after* His ministry successes. For example, after feeding the five thousand, He immediately departed for the mountain in order to pray. It was my custom for many years to invest all my prayer energy *before* ministry and, then, after ministry to "crash" (relax). But Jesus gave Himself to prayer in the natural "down time" that comes after ministry exertion. Not only did this guard Him from temptation, but it was also His opportunity to be renewed in His Father's affirmation. This was the time when the Father would tell Him, "Good job, My Son!"

It's A Pilgrimage

Living in a place where we are totally free from the praise and rejection of man is difficult to attain, and even more difficult to sustain. If my own experience in this battle is indicative of a pattern, then it seems that we never gain full victory over the specter of being touched by man's praise. We tend to wander in and out of victory's freedom in a pilgrimage sort of way.

I made an entry in my journal once that convicts me every time I read it. I don't live in the perfection of this statement, but it's something toward which I'm constantly straining. I wrote it this way: "It doesn't matter where I am, what nation I'm in, what event I'm at, what church I'm at, or how many people are there—I preach for an audience of One."

Paul's statement in 2 Corinthians 4:5 means so much to me: "For we do not preach ourselves, but Christ Jesus the Lord, and ourselves your bondservants for Jesus' sake." The Lord has shown me how easy it is for me to preach myself. Oh, don't get me wrong. I'm preaching the gospel! But I'm doing it in such a way that impresses people. It's possible for people to come away from my sermon talking about Bob Sorge. It's possible for their attention to become focused more on the vessel than the message.

Today's preachers are probably more equipped than at any other time in history. We are schooled in communications and public speaking, in oratorical skills, and in the art of preaching. Our verbal presentations are virtual master-pieces, works of art in themselves. They become so impressive that the listeners come away talking more about the speaker than about Jesus! When that happens I am no longer preaching Christ, I am preaching myself. **The true servant of Christ will guard the flourish and style with which he delivers the gospel, lest the hearers become more impressed with the preacher than with Christ Himself.**

This same principle also applies to worship leaders. Today's worship teams are without doubt the most sophisticated of all history in terms of musicianship, equipment-readiness, and professional acumen. It's possible for worshipers to come away from our services more impressed with our musicianship and smooth leadership than with the face of Christ. God help us lest we proclaim ourselves!

Can You See It?

We convince ourselves, "What's the big deal? I don't know why Bob is making such a big deal of this thing in this book. It's not a problem area for me. I don't struggle with people's praises."

We're dealing with a part of our being that we don't fully know ourselves. Jeremiah 17:9 says that we don't know the deceitful wickedness of our own hearts. Our motives are defiled in ways we don't even know yet. God alone sees the duplicity of our motivations. We cry, "God, I'm doing this *only* for Your glory!"

God says, "Oh, really?"

You can't repent of something you don't see. But God is commited to helping us see the hidden motives of our hearts. So He says, "I know you can't see it, so let Me help." And He turns up the fire! Suddenly issues start coming to the surface that we didn't even know existed in the depths of our heart. It's not until the heat is turned up that we see how much we've gained sustenance from the praise of man.

To whatever extent you are willing to admit it, there is something in all of us that enjoys the attention and praises of people. We like it when the bride of Christ notices us! But Jesus cannot entrust His bride to servants who desire the bride's affections.

To illustrate my point, I want to go to the book of Esther and look at a man by the name of Hegai. Hegai represents you and me—those of us who desire to be servant leaders that God can use for the furtherance of His kingdom purposes.

Hegai

The book of Esther tells the story of how King Ahasuerus went on a search for a bride. Many young virgins from across the land had been brought into the palace and were being prepared to meet the King. The woman of his choosing would become Queen. Esther (a Jewish maiden) was among those chosen as a possible candidate, and she underwent many months of beauty treatments in preparation for her presentation to the King. Esther ends up becoming the chosen bride, and the story of how that happens is most intriguing. Read the book of Esther!

Hegai was a eunuch in King Ahasuerus' court, and his job was to provide oversight for all the women in the King's household. When the time came to find a bride for the King, Hegai was the man in charge. Thus, Esther came directly under Hegai's care as she was being prepared to come before the King.

Now to the verse that I'm highlighting:

> *Now when the turn came for Esther the daughter of Abihail the uncle of Mordecai, who had taken her as his daughter, to go in to the king, she requested nothing but what Hegai the king's eunuch, the custodian of the women, advised. And Esther obtained favor in the sight of all who saw her* (Esther 2:15).

In ancient times, kings would surround themselves with many eunuchs. In fact, there were certain responsibilities with which eunuchs alone were entrusted. True to custom, King Ahasuerus of Persia had many eunuchs in his service, but the foremost eunuch was a man by the name of Hegai.

King Ahasuerus placed a eunuch as custodian over Esther for one very specific reason: he was safe company for the bride. As a eunuch, Hegai would have no personal desires toward Esther whom he served.

Imagine the proximity with which Hegai served Esther. He helped clothe her, he dabbled perfume on her, and he messed with her. He prepared her in a very intimate fashion without ever desiring her for himself. All that Hegai wanted was for Esther to be appealing to the King. Hegai was a faithful friend of the Bridegroom, seeking only to safeguard Esther's affections for the King and to present her as fully ready for her wedding day.

Spiritual Eunuchs

As I meditated upon Hegai's example, the Lord gave me this word, "I am raising up spiritual eunuchs in this hour." I realized this word was equally pertinent to both men and women in the body of Christ. **I understood the Lord to be saying that He was preparing leaders who would be safe company for the bride of Christ—leaders who would not desire the bride's affections and praise and attention.**

How would the Lord's leaders have this desire for man's praise cut away from their lives? I realized it would be through the surgery of a strong pruning. As the Lord's scalpel would begin to cut, leaders would begin to see issues in their hearts they've never seen before. They would be suddenly faced with the actual motivations of their hearts.

The Lord's knife is coming into the lives of His leaders, and He is removing from them the mechanism that desires the recognition of man. Because of the intensity of the cutting away that is taking place in their hearts and the excruciating nature of the pain, these leaders will become qualified to prepare the bride for Christ's return. This knife will touch within their being everything that remotely de-

sires the praise of man. Instead of desiring human affirmation and recognition, these leaders will come through the
pruning desiring only to do the pleasure of their Lord. The
King will find them worthy of the highest entrustment—to
feed, nurture, and prepare the bride for her wedding day.

The Friend Of The Bridegroom

Hegai was a true friend of the Bridegroom. He faithfully
prepared the bride for her wedding day without in any way
seeking to divert her attentions or affections to himself.

John the Baptist called himself the friend of the Bridegroom when he said, "'He who has the bride is the bridegroom; but the friend of the bridegroom, who stands and
hears him, rejoices greatly because of the bridegroom's voice.
Therefore this joy of mine is fulfilled'" (John 3:29). As the
Bridegroom's friend (or "the best man"), John the Baptist
represents the servant leader who is called by God to prepare the bride of Christ for her wedding day.

Sincere leaders in the church desire to be a true friend to
Christ. A true friend seeks to preserve the bride's affections
for none other than her Beloved. The temptation for the bride,
however, in the absence of the Bridegroom, is to start to pay
attention to the friend. The bride begins to notice the faithfulness and integrity of the friend, and she starts to give him
her grateful appreciation.

The bride says these kinds of things to the friend, "Oh
Pastor, your sermon today was *incredible*! Did you read my
mail today or what?! I mean, that was *exactly* the word that I
needed to hear today. It was so easy to understand and, yet,
so profound. Oh Pastor, I can't tell you how grateful I am to
God that I have a pastor who hears from God!"

The bride is praising the friend.

Or the bride will say to the friend, "I just love coming to
your Bible study. You make the Bible come alive! The other
Bible teachers in our church are good, but I make a point of
coming to your study every week. I hope you never close
down this group!"

Or the bride will say to the friend, "I just love it when you lead worship! There is an incredible anointing on your life to lead worship. Wow, was today's worship service ever glorious?! Why did the pastor have to preach anyways? I could have worshiped for hours! It's just not the same with the other worship leaders. It's a special anointing that God has given just to you."

Make no mistake, the bride *will* praise the friend. The issue is, what will the friend do when the bride praises him? Will he drink in her praise? If the friend starts to flirt with the bride and starts to feed off her praises, he is no longer a *friend*; he is a *competitor*.

A true friend will never infringe on the Bridegroom's sphere. The Groom's sphere is the bride's affections. He "has the bride." He holds her affections and heart. A true friend will never usurp or flirt with that which is the Bridegroom's alone—her affections.

The Weakness Of The Flesh

As I said at the beginning of this chapter, I am still not living in total victory in this area. I still find my flesh at times gratified by the attention of the bride.

When that happens, these statements would be true:

- I am in more pain now than ever over the tendency of my flesh to feed off man's praise.
- The intense pruning of God has not given me uncontested victory, but it has sensitized me greatly to the issues. Now, when the praise of man begins to allure me, I am almost immediately alerted to what's happening. My sensitivity to the entrapment of man's praise has been multiplied exponentially.
- I have been equipped by the Lord with ways to deal with the praise when it comes my way. Now I repeat my Lord's words, "I do not receive honor from men." I declare those words as that to which I am attaining.

- Because of my sensitivity, I sometimes feel like I'm doing worse in this area than ever before. But the Lord helps me to see that in fact I have matured and made great progress in His eyes. It's just that I'm living in greater light, and the brighter the light the uglier the stain appears to be.
- I have prepared myself for a lifetime journey toward victory. The victory is not so much a attainment as it is a constant embracing of the death process—dying to self.
- As I have given my heart to serving Him with purer motives in this area, I have experienced a dimension of affection from His heart to mine that is so incredible I don't know how to write about it.

Chapter 11

How Should I Praise Other People?

If you have read this book in chronological order, by now you are well aware of the snare of man's praise. A desire wells up inside of us to avoid feeding off the praise of man and to avoid causing others to stumble by praising them inordinately.

So this leads us to three very important questions which must be answered before this short book can be said to be complete:

"Should I praise other people?"

"If so, then how do I do that properly?"

"And how should I respond when others affirm and praise me?"

I hope to answer these three questions in our final two chapters.

"Should I Praise Other People?"

Here's my best answer to that question: **I do not seek the praise of other people, but I do seek to honor and affirm and encourage other believers as much as possible.** It's right that I honor others in a fitting way, but I myself should not seek the honor of people, nor should I find my identity and fulfillment in their praise. My sense of satisfaction should come from God's praise alone. In other words, **I'm not looking to get it, but I am looking to give it.**

In fact, the Scriptures reveal that I am to affirm you on a continual basis! Get a load of this list, and this is only a beginning list! But according to God's word I am called to:

- Love you.
  "'A new commandment I give to you, that you love one another; as I have loved you, that you also love one another'" (John 13:34).

- Encourage you.
  "...and sent Timothy, our brother and minister of God, and our fellow laborer in the gospel of Christ, to establish you and encourage you concerning your faith" (1 Thessalonians 3:2).

- Be kindly affectionate toward you with brotherly love.
  "Be kindly affectionate to one another with brotherly love, in honor giving preference to one another" (Romans 12:10).

- Receive you.
  "Therefore receive one another, just as Christ also received us, to the glory of God" (Romans 15:7).

- Admonish you.
  "Now I myself am confident concerning you, my brethren, that you also are full of goodness, filled with all knowledge, able also to admonish one another" (Romans 15:14).

- Be tenderhearted toward you.
  "And be kind to one another, tenderhearted, forgiving one another, just as God in Christ forgave you" (Ephesians 4:32).

- Comfort and edify you.
  "Therefore comfort each other and edify one another, just

as you also are doing" (1 Thessalonians 5:11).

- Exhort you daily—and so much the more as we see the Day approaching
  "...but exhort one another daily, while it is called 'Today,' lest any of you be hardened through the deceitfulness of sin" (Hebrews 3:13).

  "...not forsaking the assembling of ourselves together, as is the manner of some, but exhorting one another, and so much the more as you see the Day approaching (Hebrews 10:25).

- Consider you in order to stir up love and good works.
  "And let us consider one another in order to stir up love and good works" (Hebrews 10:24).

- Have compassion for you.
  "Finally, all of you be of one mind, having compassion for one another; love as brothers, be tenderhearted, be courteous" (1 Peter 3:8).

- Strengthen you.
  "'But I have prayed for you, that your faith should not fail; and when you have returned to Me, strengthen your brethren'" (Luke 22:32).

- Edify you (build you up).
  "Therefore let us pursue the things which make for peace and the things by which one may edify another" (Romans 14:19).

Furthermore, we are exhorted to give extra honor to those who serve as elders among the flock of God: "Let the elders who rule well be counted worthy of double honor, especially those who labor in the word and doctrine" (1 Timothy 5:17). So whatever honor and praise is due other believers, elders who labor in the word and doctrine are deserving of double honor and praise.

Praise, properly expressed and received, will strengthen us in our walk. God has made us to need encouragement from one another. Praise and affirmation can bolster our courage to persevere in our warfare. God knows that we have enough things coming at us (between the world, the flesh, and the devil) to constantly tear us down, weary us, discourage us, wound us, and disappoint us. In the midst of that deluge of resistance, God has intended that we help one another forward with our words.

Just as Jesus washes His bride with His word (Ephesians 5:26), we are to wash one another with our words. In fact, Hebrews 10:25 makes it clear that our affirming and building up of one another should accelerate and grow the closer we get to Christ's return. Implicit in this verse is the understanding that as the attack of Satan against believers accelerates toward the end of the very end, the endtime church will be needing the mutual edification and encouragement and praise of the body of Christ in an unparalleled way.

So not only should you be praising your brothers and sisters, you should be doing it more and more as time goes on!

Paul praised others. He referred to a brother who was praised throughout all the churches: "And we have sent with him the brother whose praise is in the gospel throughout all the churches" (2 Corinthians 8:18). And Paul also praised the believers in Corinth for their spiritual diligence: "Now I praise you, brethren, that you remember me in all things and keep the traditions just as I delivered them to you" (1 Corinthians 11:2). So Paul was not skiddish about praising man for the right reasons, in the right way.

However, he also withheld his praise from the Corinthians in connection with their abuses of corporate worship:

- *Now in giving these instructions I do not praise you, since you come together not for the better but for the worse* (1 Corinthians 11:17).
- *What! Do you not have houses to eat and drink in? Or do you despise the church of God and shame those who have nothing? What shall I say to you? Shall I praise you in this? I do not praise you* (1 Corinthians 11:22).

So there are things that we should praise in others, and then there are other things that we should not praise. This leads us to our next question. If we are to be increasing in our praise of others, how do we know what to praise them for and what not to praise them for? When and how do we do this in a kingdom manner?

"How Should I Affirm Others?"

This becomes a very important question because if I am to praise and affirm and build you up, then *how* do I do that without fueling your carnality? To put it another way, since I don't want you to feed off my praise in a way that dishonors the Lord, how do I affirm you without doing you a disservice?

This much I know: we're not called to keep each other low. Our calling is to build each other up. It's God's job to keep you humble as needed; it's my job to praise and encourage you.

When I encourage you, it's not my concern how you handle that. You might respond perfectly, or you might allow my praise to inflate your flesh. Your response is not my jurisdiction; my only concern is to be faithful before God to encourage you.

So, dear saints: let the praises fly! Affirm and encourage one another! But now to the *how* question.

First of all, in looking at Paul's example, we learn that praise and encouragement must be given with discernment. Paul praised the Corinthians for some things (1 Corinthians 11:2, cited above), but there were some things for which he did not praise them (1 Corinthians 11:17,22, also cited above). So we do not praise others indiscriminately, but rather selectively and carefully.

Jesus, who was very discriminating with His praise, gave us the pattern for how to praise others. I studied how Jesus praised His disciples, and the incidents were few indeed. Jesus did not gush forth praises on His disciples just to keep them propped up emotionally. When He praised them, it was very strategic.

The most significant occurrence of Jesus praising His disciples is in the following passage:

> *He said to them, "But who do you say that I am?" Simon*
> *Peter answered and said, "You are the Christ, the Son of*
> *the living God." Jesus answered and said to him, "Blessed*
> *are you, Simon Bar-Jonah, for flesh and blood has not re-*
> *vealed this to you, but My Father who is in heaven" (Mat-*
> *thew 16:15-17).*

Notice this: **Jesus commended Peter by affirming the work of God in Peter.** Jesus was saying, "There! That's the Father! You're getting it Peter! How blessed you are, for now you're receiving grace and revelation from heaven. This is the work of God in you."

Jesus never complimented them for things done in the strength of their flesh. "For we are the circumcision, who worship God in the Spirit, rejoice in Christ Jesus, and have no confidence in the flesh" (Philippians 3:3). So here's the principle Jesus modelled for us: **Affirm what <u>God</u> is doing in someone by His grace.**

The Good, The Bad, The Ugly

Sometimes, when we see someone's shortcomings, we have difficulty giving proper recognition to their moments of Holy Spirit inspiration. Let me explain.

In the story cited above, Peter gets a divine revelation of Jesus' identity, and Jesus affirms the authenticity of that revelation. The context of that statement is very important, however. It's in the very next paragraph, just moments later, that we see a dramatically different side of Peter:

> *From that time Jesus began to show to His disciples that*
> *He must go to Jerusalem, and suffer many things from the*
> *elders and chief priests and scribes, and be killed, and be*
> *raised the third day. Then Peter took Him aside and began*
> *to rebuke Him, saying, "Far be it from You, Lord; this shall*

not happen to You!" But He turned and said to Peter, "Get behind Me, Satan! You are an offense to Me, for you are not mindful of the things of God, but the things of men" (Matthew 16:21-23).

In verse 16, Peter is getting direct revelation from the Father; in verse 22, Peter is a mouthpiece for Satan. Talk about a roller coaster ride! From the heights to the depths in mere minutes!

Knowing Peter's frailty, I'm not surprised to hear Jesus say to Peter, "Get behind Me, Satan!" What's surprising is to hear Jesus say to the same man, "Blessed are you, Simon Bar-Jonah, for flesh and blood has not revealed this to you, but My Father who is in heaven."

Jesus had the incredible ability, while fully seeing and knowing Peter's weakness, to still praise that which was truly of God in his life. I'm not always like that. Sometimes I think, "I'm not going to tell you how anointed you were just now because I know there are evil things still lurking in your heart." But when Jesus saw the Father's hand at work, He affirmed that.

The point: We should affirm what God is doing in those around us, even when we see their shortcomings.

How Paul Praised Others

Paul consistently employed a method of encouragement which balances all these considerations. He used this form of encouragement over and over in his epistles, and here's just one instance: "We are bound to thank God always for you, brethren, as it is fitting, because your faith grows exceedingly, and the love of every one of you all abounds toward each other" (2 Thessalonians 1:3).

In this verse, Paul praised the believers at Thessalonica for their growing faith and for their abundant love for each other. However, instead of giving them the credit, he gave the credit to God. He said, "We...thank God...because your faith grows exceedingly." He gave thanks to God because he realized their growth in faith and love was only because of God's grace manifest in their lives. **So with one simple phrase Paul did two things: he praised their spiritual attainments, and He gave all the credit to God.**

Notice this same pattern of simultaneously giving thanks to God and praise to the believers throughout his epistles:

- *First, I thank my God through Jesus Christ for you all, that your faith is spoken of throughout the whole world* (Romans 1:8).
- *I thank my God always concerning you for the grace of God which was given to you by Christ Jesus, that you were enriched in everything by Him in all utterance and all knowledge* (1 Corinthians 1:4-5).
- *We give thanks to the God and Father of our Lord Jesus Christ, praying always for you, since we heard of your faith in Christ Jesus and of your love for all the saints* (Colossians 1:3-4).
- *We give thanks to God always for you all, making mention of you in our prayers, remembering without ceasing your work of faith, labor of love, and patience of hope in our Lord Jesus Christ in the sight of our God and Father* (1 Thessalonians 1:2-3).
- *I thank God, whom I serve with a pure conscience, as my forefathers did, as without ceasing I remember you in my prayers night and day...when I call to remembrance the genuine faith that is in you, which dwelt first in your grandmother Lois and your mother Eunice, and I am persuaded is in you also* (2 Timothy 1:3,5).
- *I thank my God, making mention of you always in my prayers, hearing of your love and faith which you have toward the Lord Jesus and toward all the saints* (Philemon 1:4-5).

In each of these epistle portions, Paul praises the believers for their obedience to the faith while also ascribing all the credit to the grace of God at work in them.

Therefore, based upon Paul's model, when you want to praise or encourage someone else for the grace of God at work in their lives, you can say things like, "I thank God for the way He uses you to minister His word." "I thank God for the sacrificial way you serve and love the children of this church." "I am so thankful to God that you were obedient to share your heart in our small group meeting with such openness and conviction." "I am so grateful to God for the passion He has given you for Jesus. It inspires our whole church!"

As a father, this became very important to me: how do I affirm my children in a godly fashion? I want to compliment them, but I don't want to build their vanity. I want to affirm them, but I don't want to build their pride and self-sufficiency. How do I praise them without causing them to put their confidence in the flesh? The answer for me was this: praise and build them up by showing them how God is enabling them to fulfill their accomplishments. Now I say to them things like, "With a wonderful report card like this, do you realize how much God is helping you? The hand of the Lord is upon you!" Or I might say, "Sweetheart, you are so beautiful — God is making you into a truly beautiful woman of God."

I want my kids to feel edified by me as their father, but I also want them to realize that anything and everything good in their lives has come to them through the grace of God and not through any inherent goodness of their own. Paul's example has helped me so much in this area.

Come with me now to our final chapter as we ask a very difficult question, "How should I respond when others praise me?"

Chapter 12

How Should I Respond When Praised?

Now, we affirmed in Chapter Six that the praise of man is a snare. And we also gave four reasons in Chapter Nine why it is absolutely vital that we gain victory over the desire for man's praise:

1. God cannot entrust the higher dimensions of kingdom authority and power to vessels that are nurtured by the praise of man.
2. When we feed off the praise of man, we are actually succumbing to idolatry—finding our sustenance in something other than Christ Himself.
3. It is only as we are free from wanting to impress people and seek to honor God alone in our ministries that we will be able to find true accuracy in spiritual warfare, where our ministry truly "hits the mark."
4. Those who are not touched by the praise of man become free of all men. They are free to love all men equally and completely, regardless of whether they are rejected or loved in return. It's the place of total freedom.

It is our desire, therefore, to be completely free from the praise of man. But we are now presented with a problem, for we have just finished saying that we should be praising and encouraging and affirming one another on an increasing basis. We have no problem as long as we're giving out the praise. The problem comes when we are suddenly the recipient of the praise.

How are we to hold our hearts before God when others praise us? How do we respond in a way that pleases the heart of the Father, so that He can release us into higher dimensions of kingdom effectiveness? How can we guard our hearts so that our beloved Lord is delighted with us?

"What Should I Do When Others Affirm Me?"

So this is our next and concluding question. What do I do when another believer, in a genuine effort to encourage and edify me, praises and honors me for something I've done?

Here's where the fire is. Once you're sensitized to this whole dynamic of not receiving the praise of man, there comes an immediate fire into your soul when someone compliments you. You're like, "O God, what do I do now? I don't want to feed off this praise! But this sister is so sincere, I don't want to be rude either." This fire is what Proverbs 27:21 is pointing to: "The crucible is for silver and the furnace for gold, and a man is tested by the praise accorded him" (NAS). When someone praises you, the fire is turned high, and the true attitudes of your heart begin to surface. God will use the compliments you receive to show you your heart.

For example, someone says to you, "There was an incredible anointing on you when you sang that song! Wow, I haven't seen that kind of anointing on a solo in a long time." On the outside you demur with a quiet smile and say, "Praise God." But on the inside you're going through an inner battle, "I don't receive this praise, Lord! I'm not going to feed off this! Why is this person doing this to me right now??"

So I'm fine with giving out praise, I just don't know what to do when it comes my way. I don't know what words to say; I don't know how big to smile; I'm not sure what to do with my hands; I'm upset at the way my flesh is enjoying the compliment. This person thinks they're edifying me, but instead they've triggered a fiery battle within my soul.

I went to the Lord in prayer about this struggle because I was in a dilemma. I knew it was scriptural for others to praise me, but I didn't know what to do when it came my way. I didn't want to receive the praise, but I also didn't want to be ungracious or distant.

The answer came to me from Romans 15:7, "Therefore receive one another, just as Christ also received us, to the glory of God." Here's the principle I saw:

When you praise me, I do not receive <u>your praise</u>, I receive <u>you</u>.

I don't receive your praise because it is simply the opinion of man. But I receive you, because I realize that in praising me you're simply trying to express your love for me.

So when someone praises me, my response now is typically, "Thank you for your love!" And I'll offer an appropriate sign of affection, such as a squeeze on that person's arm or an embrace or a warm smile. Even though I'm not receiving that person's praise, I am receiving that person and his or her love.

This is why we are to praise and encourage one another—that we might *receive* one another.

If someone undergoes a liver transplant, the doctors might say, "His body has received the new liver." Or they might say, "His body rejected the new liver." When the members of the body don't receive another member, the body is in serious trouble. It is critically important to the health and wholeness of the body that it receive each and every member.

The same is true in the body of Christ. The body of Christ will never come to full maturity and fruitfulness until we receive each other as equal members of the body. The Lord intends that we open our hearts wide to one another (see 2 Corinthians 6:11-13).

So when someone encourages or affirms you, give praise to God for His grace manifest in and through your life. And then receive your brother or sister in holy Christian affection!

Conclusion

In conclusion, perhaps it may be helpful to review sequentially the major principles which we have explored in this book:

1.   All of us will know rejection until our dying day. It's an unavoidable dynamic of our human existence.
2.   No one knows rejection better than Jesus. Jesus proved that even if you're perfect you'll be rejected.
3.   The more like Jesus you become, the more rejected you'll be.
4.   If we respond properly to rejection, we gain eternal treasure.
5.   Rejection is one of God's specialty tools in the school of the Spirit, reserved for those He especially likes.
6.   Rejection is a trial—but the acceptance of the Father is the healing ointment.
7.   Rejection stings, but it doesn't have to wound your heart.
8.   We must forgive those who reject us.
9.   We must learn to believe and receive the Father's love.
10. When God accepts me, I need acceptance from no one else.
11. Although I need only God's acceptance, I desperately need proper relationship and connection to my brothers and sisters in Christ.
12. One of the greatest challenges of Christian maturity is to make myself vulnerable to your kindness

and affection, while not allowing myself to be wounded by your rejection.

13. It's a sign of maturity when we can receive correction without interpreting it as rejection.
14. You won't be healed of rejection by analyzing the source of your rejection, but by looking at your source of acceptance. Whose acceptance do you seek?
15. When I yearn for your acceptance, I open myself to your rejection.
16. You cannot seek the acceptance of both God and man.
17. Rejection and praise are opposite ends of the same continuum with identical root issues.
18. Two reasons why we should not be touched by the praise of man: people are undependable, and the opinions of people are insignificant.
19. The fear of man (the desire for man's praise) is a snare.
20. Jesus did not receive the honor man.
21. When we're energized by men's praises, we lose our discernment.
22. Don't receive the cheap replacement of man's praise when you can contend for the highest praise—the honor of God Himself.
23. To feed off the honor of man is idolatry.
24. When I no longer receive the praise of man, I become free of all men—free, that is, to love all men equally and unconditionally.
25. Living in a place where we are totally free from the praise and rejection of man is a lifetime pilgrimage.
26. I do not seek the praise of other people, but I do seek to honor and encourage other believers as much as possible.
27. I can praise others by giving thanks to God for what His grace has accomplished in their lives.
28. We should affirm what God is doing in those around us, even when we see their shortcomings.

29.   When you praise me, I do not receive *your praise*, I receive *you*.

Let us pray. *Holy Father, we bless You for Your un-fathomable love. You accept us totally and uncondition-ally. We are healed and made whole in Your affections. Grant us might through Your Spirit in our inner being that we might know this love, that we might be filled with all the fullness of God. Set us free—free from the wounds of man's rejections, and free from the allurements of man's praises. Join us in passionate love to our brothers and sis-ters, empower us to love others as Christ loves them, and may we be satisfied with Your approval of our lives. We ask these things in the name of our beloved Lord Jesus Christ. Amen!*

Order Form

Books by Bob Sorge
(Book descriptions on next page)

	Qty.	Price	Total
BOOKS:			
ENVY: THE ENEMY WITHIN	____	$12.00	____
SECRETS OF THE SECRET PLACE	____	$13.00	____
GLORY: When Heaven Invades Earth	____	$ 9.00	____
PAIN, PERPLEXITY & PROMOTION	____	$13.00	____
THE FIRE OF GOD'S LOVE	____	$12.00	____
THE FIRE OF DELAYED ANSWERS	____	$13.00	____
IN HIS FACE: A Prophetic Call to Renewed Focus	____	$12.00	____
EXPLORING WORSHIP: A Practical Guide to Praise and Worship	____	$15.00	____
Exploring Worship WORKBOOK & DISCUSSION GUIDE	____	$ 5.00	____
DEALING WITH THE REJECTION AND PRAISE OF MAN	____	$ 9.00	____

SPECIAL PACKET #3
One of each book ____ $79.00 ____
    (Special Packet Includes Free Shipping)

Subtotal		____
Shipping, Add 10% (Minimum of $2.00)		____
Missouri Residents Add 7.35% Sales Tax		____
Total Enclosed		____

U.S. Funds Only

Send payment with order to: Oasis House
                                P.O. Box 127
                                Greenwood, MO 64034-0127

Name _____

Address: Street _____

             City _____ State _____

             Zip _____

For MasterCard/VISA orders and quantity discounts,
call 816-623-9050

Or order on our fully secure website:
www.oasishouse.net

Description of Resources on the Previous Page

- ❖ ENVY: THE ENEMY WITHIN — This short but gripping book reveals how ambitious motives and carnal comparisons between ministries can hinder the release of God's blessings. Explore how 2-talent saints envy 5-talent saints. Riveting, provocative, and controversial.

- ❖ THE FIRE OF GOD'S LOVE compels us toward the passionate love that God is producing within the bride in this hour for her Bridegroom, the Lord Jesus.

- ❖ GLORY: WHEN HEAVEN INVADES EARTH articulates the highest goal of worship—to behold the Glory of God! Be renewed in the assurance that God's Glory is coming, and let your vision be kindled for a personal, life-changing encounter with God Himself.

- ❖ PAIN, PERPLEXITY & PROMOTION looks at the book of Job from a fresh, prophetic vantage. Job's life shows how God promotes His chosen vessels to higher heights than they would have conceived possible. Let Job's example compel you toward God's highest and best!

- ❖ THE FIRE OF DELAYED ANSWERS explores how God sometimes delays the answers to our prayers in order to produce godly character in us. This book is "spiritual food" for those in crisis or difficulty.

- ❖ IN HIS FACE propels the reader passionately toward a more personal and intimate relationship with Jesus Christ. Challenging devotional reading.

- ❖ EXPLORING WORSHIP is a 300-page textbook that covers a full range of subjects related to praise and worship. Translated into several languages, this bestselling book is being used internationally as a text by many Bible colleges, Bible study groups, and worship leading teams. Also available is an accompanying WORKBOOK/DISCUSSION GUIDE.

- ❖ SECRETS OF THE SECRET PLACE — Bob shares some of the secrets he's learned in making the secret place energizing and delightful. This has become Bob's bestseller. Gain fresh fuel for your secret devotional life with God!